FUN WITH
PHYSICS

by
Susan McGrath

BOOKS FOR WORLD EXPLORERS
NATIONAL GEOGRAPHIC SOCIETY

Contents

Copyright © 1986
National Geographic Society
Library of Congress CIP data 104
Second Printing 1988

Introduction

"All aboard!" You've been standing in line for half an hour, gripping your ticket and listening to the whoops and screams of the roller-coaster passengers overhead. Now it's your turn. You settle into your seat. The car lurches forward. A chain pulls your car to the top of the first steep rise. At this moment, you're *probably* not thinking about physics. But watch how many examples of physics you'll experience—and don't worry about all the terms in **bold type.** You'll hear more about them later.

The moving chain runs on electricity. By pulling you to the top of an incline, the chain converts electrical energy to gravitational **potential energy**—stored energy you have when you're in a position to fall. Then **gravity** tugs on you. You're swooping down the steep incline, converting your potential energy to **kinetic energy**—the energy you have when you are moving.

At the top of each incline, you feel weightless. That's because your **inertia** keeps your body going up momentarily as the car hurries downward. Suddenly, the car enters a steeply banked turn. You feel as if you might be tipped out of your seat. Actually, the tilted track forces the car to turn, pushing against the car with **centripetal force.** If it weren't for the tilt, your car would go straight and jump the tracks.

Whooaa! The car enters a loop and you're upside down! You have to travel fast for this to work. Why don't you fall out? Inertia and centripetal force are at work again. Inertia tries to keep you moving outward in a straight line. The track acts against inertia with centripetal force and pushes the car around in a circle. Inertia presses you into your car, even when it's upside down.

Now the inclines are getting smaller. The roller coaster is slowing down. **Friction** works to slow you to a stop. Whew!

If you like roller coasters, then you felt right at home on this ride. But did some of the terms in heavy type look like Greek to you? They refer to principles of physics. Actually, many physics terms come from Greek. The word "physics" itself comes from a Greek word meaning "nature."

Physics is the study of energy and matter—and that covers just about everything under, and including, the sun. If physics does not seem to relate to you, just think: Physics explains sound to musicians, color to artists, jumping to basketball players, speed

*Thrill seekers feel weightless for a split second at Six Flags Over Texas, a park near Dallas. At the top of the hump, riders keep going up for a bit after their car has headed down. That's because of **inertia,** which you'll read more about on page 38.*

HANK MORGAN/RAINBOW

to race-car drivers, light to photographers, ice cream to ice-cream makers. This book divides physics into four parts and shows how it relates to your life: physics of fun, physics of the natural world, physics at home, and physics of sports. You'll find important terms printed in **bold type.** They also appear—with definitions—in the glossary, at the back of the book.

You'll be amazed at what physics explains. But don't stop with what you read. Follow the "Try It!" suggestions throughout the book, and do the activities at the end of each chapter. You'll soon understand a lot more about physics. Then the next time you're waiting for a roller-coaster ride, watch physics at work as the cars roll over the tracks. You'll know more about what's happening.

The roller coaster cars go all the way up and over. The riders, completely upside down, remain in their seats. **Centripetal force** *and inertia keep everybody safely seated. Physics explains centripetal force (see page 89) and inertia—plus a lot of tricks that once seemed mysterious or magical. To capture this scene, the photographer used a wide-angle lens. It makes the loops appear to be leaning, even though they're not.*

1
PHYSICS
of
FUN

You probably took your first ride on a swing when you were so little you can't even remember it. Now it's just . . . get on the swing and go. You lean back and lift your legs to go forward. You lean forward and drop your legs to swing back. Why does leaning and pumping your legs help you swing? It's physics!

As you swing your legs forward and raise them, you are using energy of motion. Physicists call it **kinetic** (kuh-NET-ik) **energy.** When you hold your legs in that position as the swing changes direction, the kinetic energy momentarily changes to stored energy, called **potential** (puh-TEN-shul) **energy.** Drop your legs and the potential energy changes back to kinetic energy. It helps push you back in the reverse direction. On the downswing, **gravity** helps give you speed.

The swing rocks to and fro in an arc. Physicists call this motion **simple harmonic motion.** To illustrate simple harmonic motion, a photographer attached six small lights to Amy Blechman, 13 (left), of San Mateo, California. Then he exposed the film for a bit longer than usual. Here, during the long exposure, the lights draw arcs in the air as Amy swings. "If physics is swinging," says Amy, "then physics is fun."

Friction: Life would be tough without it. Friction helps keep cars from skidding off roads. It keeps nails and screws from slipping out of walls. It lets you walk without sliding.

Friction is the force that acts when two surfaces rub against each other. It helps you in many ways, but it also slows you down and produces heat. Friction between you and the air slows you down when you're riding your bike. By bending forward over the handlebars, you help reduce air friction against your body. Friction between the parts of a car engine heats them up. People use lubricants to reduce that friction. The most common lubricant is oil. Pour oil between two moving parts and their surfaces will rub against the oil rather than against each other. The oil is slippery and smooth. It allows parts to move—without overheating.

Nature's Brakes

WILLIAM DEKAY

◀ *Seated on nylon mats, visitors breeze down a giant fiberglass slide in an amusement park in Estes Park, Colorado. The slick mats make the rides faster, because the mats slide on the fiberglass more easily than the visitors' clothing would. A physicist would tell you that the mats reduce the* **friction** *between the people and the slide. Friction is a force that occurs when one object rubs against another. This force slows things down.*

Try it!

For handmade friction, rub your palms together hard. The heat you'll feel is the result of friction. Try putting lotion or talcum powder on your hands and rubbing them again. Lotion and powder act as lubricants. Your hands should slide more easily and therefore produce less heat.

LOEL BARR

▲ *Before setting off, Robbie Peirce, 14, of Washington, D. C., checks the adjustment of his bicycle brakes. Hand brakes work by friction. When you squeeze the brakes, cables press small rubber pads against the rims of your front and back wheels. Friction between the rubber pads and the metal rims slows you down. Next time you're on your bike, feel the pads after braking to a stop. The slight heat is a product of friction.*

Up, Up, Up, and Away

Airplane designers learned a bit about their business by looking at birds. Next time you see an airplane up close, take a careful look at its wings. You'll see that they have the same shape as a bird's wings (below). They are flat underneath and curved on top. The curves on top give wings their lifting power.

A wing splits the air. Some air goes over the wing. Some air goes under. Both airstreams meet at nearly the same time on the other side. Because the air going over the wing curves and travels farther, it must speed up to arrive at the rear of the wing at almost the same instant as the air below. The slower air below the wing pushes upward more than the faster air above the wing pushes down. This difference in pressure causes the wing to rise.

In 1738, a Swiss scientist named Daniel Bernoulli discovered the relationship between fast-moving fluids and pressure. (Scientists classify both air and water as fluids.) **Bernoulli's principle**

Holding tight to her kite string, Suzanna Dennis, 8, of Lagunitas, California, runs into the wind. Like air over a bird's wings, air passing over the kite presses on it less than air passing under it. The greater air pressure below the kite helps the wind push the kite up, where it will fly at the end of Suzanna's string.

A sea gull soars by the same physical principle that helps an airplane fly. Notice the shape of this gull's wings. The tops are curved. Arrows show the path that air takes as it moves past the wings. The curved paths over the wings are longer than the straight paths under them. Air following the longer, curved paths flows faster past the wings. The faster air puts less pressure on the wings than the slower air does. That's called **Bernoulli's principle.** The greater pressure under the wings creates an upward force called **lift.**

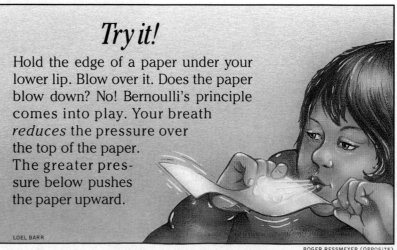

Try it!

Hold the edge of a paper under your lower lip. Blow over it. Does the paper blow down? No! Bernoulli's principle comes into play. Your breath *reduces* the pressure over the top of the paper. The greater pressure below pushes the paper upward.

states: The pressure in a fluid decreases when the fluid speeds up. Applied to airplanes, the principle explains why the slower-moving air under a wing gives the wing an upward force, or **lift.**

Long or wide wings get more lift than short or narrow ones. Fast-moving wings get more lift than slow-moving ones. Fighter jets move very fast. They need only short wings. Gliders—planes without motors—move more slowly. They need long wings.

The children at right aren't getting lift from curved wings, but Bernoulli's principle is still helping them stay aloft. They're riding a jet stream of air coming through the floor of this flying room in Nevada. The stream pushes them up, against the force of gravity, just as a strong wind might blow you off your feet. The higher pressure in the still air around the edge of the room pushes them in toward the center of the fast-moving airstream. This action is Bernoulli's principle at work. The result? The children soar in midair.

The original flying chamber like this one was designed by a Canadian sky diver who loved to fly. He figured other people would, too—and without going too far above the ground.

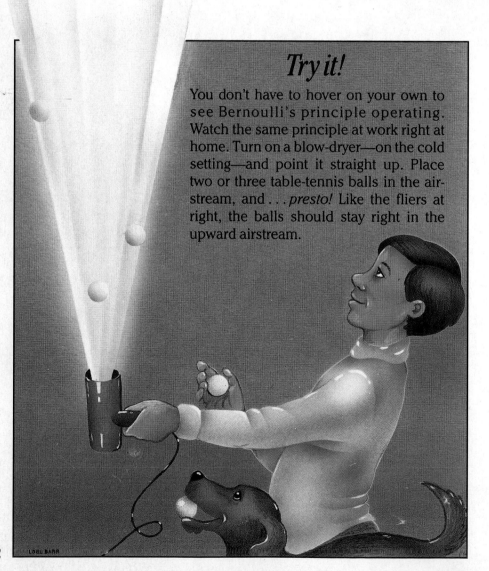

Try it!

You don't have to hover on your own to see Bernoulli's principle operating. Watch the same principle at work right at home. Turn on a blow-dryer—on the cold setting—and point it straight up. Place two or three table-tennis balls in the airstream, and . . . *presto!* Like the fliers at right, the balls should stay right in the upward airstream.

Blowing in the breeze, visitors hover in the Flyaway, a padded room designed for high-flying fun, in Las Vegas, Nevada. Under the wire-mesh floor, a propeller sends up a powerful jet of air. That wind sweeps the visitors off their feet, balancing them in midair against the downward force of gravity. Why don't they fly off to the sides? It's because of Bernoulli's principle. The fast-moving airstream is surrounded by still air. The moving airstream pushes outward with less pressure than the still air pushes inward. If a flier drifts toward the edge of the airstream, the still air pushes the flier back into it.

© PETER MENZEL 1985

12

What Floating Is All About

It's a hot day, so what do you do? You drop a few ice cubes into your glass of lemonade. Oops! You add too many and your glass overflows. When you added the ice cubes, they displaced, or pushed aside, the liquid that had occupied their space.

Displacement is important. It's what determines whether an object will float or sink. Any object dropped into a liquid displaces some of the liquid. A floating object weighs the same as the water it displaces. A sinking object weighs *more* than the water it displaces.

The ability of an object to float is called **buoyancy** (BOY-un-see). Buoyancy doesn't depend only on weight or only on shape. It depends on both. That's why a small, rounded, one-pound rock can sink while a long, wide, hundred-thousand-ton supertanker floats. The one-pound rock displaces water that weighs less than it does, so it sinks. The weight of the hundred-thousand-ton steel ship is spread out so that the ship displaces water that weighs as much as the ship. Therefore, the ship floats.

Hot-air balloons stay in the air for the same reason that huge

▶ *Six friends drift lazily on a Pennsylvania river. Their inner tubes have a lot of* **buoyancy,** *which means the tubes float easily. An object's buoyancy depends on its weight and its shape. Filled with air, the inner tubes are large, but light for their size. Empty and folded up, the tubes would be heavy for their size, and they'd sink.*

STEPHEN R. WAGNER

◀ *Why does a steel ball sink while a steel cup of the same weight floats?* **1.** *Examine what happens when you have a 2-pound (1 kg)* steel ball and a beaker filled with water.* **2.** *If you drop the ball into the*
**Metric figures in this book have been rounded off.*

beaker, the displaced water will overflow into the dish. The displaced water weighs less than the ball, and the ball sinks. **3.** *Starting over, you place an empty 2-pound steel cup in the beaker filled to the*

top. The cup displaces exactly its own weight—2 pounds of water— and floats. Any floating object displaces a volume, or an amount, of water that weighs exactly what the object weighs.

tankers float. The balloons literally float in air, just as ships float in water. Here you have to think like a physicist. As you read on page 10, physicists classify both air and water as fluids. A hot-air balloon displaces the fluid—air—in which it floats, just as a ship displaces the fluid—water—in which it floats.

How does a hot-air balloon rise in the first place? The crew must make it weigh not just the *same* as the air it displaces. They must make it weigh *less*. They do that by heating the air inside the balloon. Air expands when it is heated. Any amount of hot air weighs less than the same amount of cold air. When the crew heats the air in the balloon, the air becomes lighter and lighter in comparison with the colder air it displaces. Eventually, like a bubble in water, the balloon becomes light enough to rise. It stops rising when the weight of its basket, its crew, and its air equals the weight of the air the balloon displaces.

◀ *Hot-air balloons crowd the sky over Albuquerque, New Mexico. To remain aloft at one height, a balloon filled with hot air must weigh the same as the colder air that it displaces. A floating hot-air balloon displaces air exactly as a floating boat displaces water.*

NATIONAL GEOGRAPHIC PHOTOGRAPHER DAVID ALAN HARVEY (ABOVE)

◀ *Erin Scott Harvey, 11, and his mother, of Richmond, Virginia, exhale streams of air bubbles. The rising bubbles act just like hot-air balloons that are rising. Each bubble or balloon weighs less than the amount of fluid—water or air—that it displaces.*

Sticky Issues

When many people hear the word **adhesion** (add-HEE-zhun), they think of adhesive tape. Adhesive tape sticks. You use it to attach bandages to yourself.

Adhesion is the force of attraction between two different substances. You might call it stickiness. It occurs, for example, between sand and water. When you wet sand, adhesion occurs between the **molecules**—very tiny parts—of sand and the molecules of water. The water sticks to the sand, coating each grain.

There's a second force of attraction taking place when you wet sand. It's called **cohesion.** Cohesion is the force of attraction between molecules of the same substance. Cohesion, for example, causes the water molecules that coat one grain of sand to stick to the water molecules coating other grains. This action seems to glue the grains of sand into a firm, damp sand cake.

Water doesn't *feel* sticky, as glue and other, stronger adhesives do. But it has its sticky qualities. Watch raindrops roll down a

Contestants put the finishing touches on their entry in a sand-sculpture contest in Cannon Beach, Oregon. If you've ever tried to build a sand castle—or a sand dog—you know that dry sand doesn't work. It must be wet. That's because thin layers of water around the grains of sand act like glue, holding the sand together. When this "glue" dries, your sand castle begins to crumble.

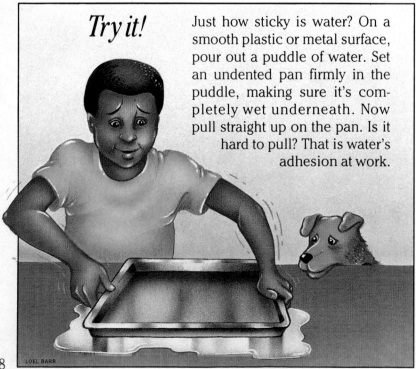

Try it!

Just how sticky is water? On a smooth plastic or metal surface, pour out a puddle of water. Set an undented pan firmly in the puddle, making sure it's completely wet underneath. Now pull straight up on the pan. Is it hard to pull? That is water's adhesion at work.

LOEL BARR

windowpane. As a drop runs down the glass, it leaves a damp trail behind it. That's adhesion at work: water sticking to the pane. But most of the drop stays together. It may even combine with another drop. Drops sticking together show cohesion at work. Cohesion in water is so strong that a drop tends to pull itself together. That's why a drop on a windowpane bulges rather than spreading out in a thin layer.

A water drop isn't the only place you can see cohesion holding water together tightly. If you fill a glass too full of water, you'll clearly observe the water bulging over the top without spilling. (Try the activity on page 33.) Water holds together at its surface with a kind of rubbery "skin." This tendency of a liquid to form a skin is called **surface tension.**

In the woods, you're likely to see another example of water's surface tension. On a quiet pond, you'll probably see insects walking right on *top* of the water, thanks to surface tension.

◄ *At the Exploratorium, a science museum in San Francisco, California, museum aide Scott Shanks pulls a giant soap bubble over Elizabeth Mertl, 5, of Burlingame, California. (Find the recipe for such a bubble on page 32.) Why does soapy water make larger, longer-lasting bubbles than fresh water does? The soap weakens the* **surface tension** *of water, the skinlike quality that holds the surface of water together. The weakened surface can stretch into fantastic shapes.*

RICHARD J. QUATAERT/FOLIO INC.

Try it!

See surface tension in action. Get some paper clips and a bowl of water. Half unfold one clip as a tool. Rest another paper clip on the tool. Gently lay the clip flat on the water. Use care so the surface tension holds it up. How do you know the clip isn't floating? *Stand* a second clip on the water. Does it float?

LOEL BARR

▲ *Why do water droplets on a violet look almost perfectly round? It's because the water molecules in a drop have a strong attraction for each other. They tug at the water on the drop's surface. The surface is pulled tight around the drop and acts like a stretchy skin. Physicists call this tendency to form an elastic skin surface tension. Some animals take advantage of water's surface tension. Have you ever seen a water strider? The long-legged insect skitters over the surface of water. It walks on the water's rubbery skin without even wetting its feet.*

Expanding Gases

Fireworks shoot into the air and popcorn pops for the same reason. Heat in each causes a gas to form that is many, many times the size of the substance from which it comes.

Why does a substance expand when it changes into a gas? Molecules of a solid or liquid are always moving, at least a bit. Add heat and the molecules move faster. They bounce around, forcing themselves farther apart. As the molecules spread, the substance expands. With enough heat, it becomes a gas.

Heated water, expanding into steam, enlarges to more than a thousand times its original size. You can sense that from observing your kitchen kettle. Steam from just half a kettle of water will keep the whistle blowing for a long time as the water boils away.

After a fireworks technician lights a fuse on a rocket, gunpowder inside the rocket catches fire and explodes. Hot gases given off by the exploding gunpowder push on the inside of the rocket and escape downward from the back end. The rocket shoots upward. Overhead, it bursts, firing colored particles across the sky.

Fourth of July fireworks burst above the Capitol and the Lincoln Memorial, in Washington, D. C. Gunpowder ignited in the rockets of the fireworks turns into hot gases and undergoes enormous expansion. The pressure produced by the expanding gases causes the rockets to shoot into the air.

Exploding out of hot cooking oil, a kernel of corn pops into a crunchy snack. The photographer used a light that flashed five times very quickly to capture the action in one picture. A raw popcorn kernel consists of white starch in a tough yellowish hull. When you heat the kernel, the tiny amount of water in the starch heats up. The heat makes the water molecules start to jiggle and spread apart. In seconds, the water has turned to steam, which needs much more room than the liquid water did. Steam pressure builds in the kernel. Suddenly, pop! The kernel bursts, releasing the steam. It spills fluffy white starch— and the popcorn goes flying.

22

Toss a pebble into a pond and you'll see ripples spread outward from the spot where the stone hit the water. Strike a gong and the air around it ripples, too. Sound waves spread out in all directions away from the gong.

Scientists call sound waves **compressional waves.** Here's how they work. When you hit the gong, it vibrates. Each time the gong vibrates outward, it whacks the air molecules next to it, transferring a pulse of kinetic energy to the air molecules and shoving them away. They don't go far before they bump into the air molecules next to them, and those bump into the next molecules, and so on. This process transfers the original pulse of energy away from the gong. Meanwhile, the vibrating gong reverses direction. This leaves a space behind the first pulse of energy, and the air molecules spread out again.

Every tiny vibration of the gong sets off an energetic wave of collisions followed by a calm, relatively empty space. The compressed, or crowded, part of the sound wave is called a **compression.** The space between compressions is called a **rarefaction** (rare-uh-FAK-shun). Each wavelength of sound consists of a single compression and a single rarefaction. When these vibrations in the air reach your ears, the tiny organs within your ears interpret them as sound.

*Music pours out of drums and tubas as a marching band plays in Madison, Wisconsin. Lines drawn around one of the tubas show that sound waves spread in all directions from their source. The source of a sound, such as a tuba, produces vibrations. The vibrations push and pull at the air, causing groups of air molecules to be compressed and expanded. Sound waves are called **compressional waves.***

Good Vibrations

Ripples fan out where a pebble plopped into a pond. Sound waves travel away from their source in a similar pattern. Sound waves, however, don't travel on a flat surface, as waves of water do. Sound waves travel in all directions, like invisible balls that grow larger and larger.

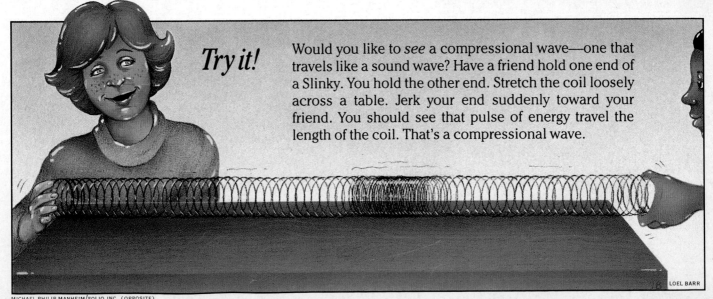

Try it! Would you like to *see* a compressional wave—one that travels like a sound wave? Have a friend hold one end of a Slinky. You hold the other end. Stretch the coil loosely across a table. Jerk your end suddenly toward your friend. You should see that pulse of energy travel the length of the coil. That's a compressional wave.

LOEL BARR

Light That Hits the Spot

In the hands of a surgeon, a beam of laser light moves across a bleeding wound and the bleeding stops. At a clothing factory, laser light cleanly cuts out shapes through mounds of fabric. Laser lights remove the shells from peanuts; they pierce holes in needles; they split diamonds; they read the prices on groceries.

Laser lights get their power through teamwork. Like members of a marching band, light waves emerge from a laser perfectly in step with one another. Light organized in this way is called **coherent** (ko-HEAR-unt) **light.** Coherent light waves, since they travel in step, join together and strengthen each other. (Waves of **incoherent light,** such as those from a flashlight, are not in step. They shine less brightly, and fade more quickly.)

Light and sound both travel in waves. However, sound can travel only by moving the molecules of a substance, such as water or air. Sound can't exist in a vacuum. Light, on the other hand, exists as tiny packets of energy called **photons.** Light can travel through airless space since it doesn't need to vibrate its surroundings to go from one place to another.

▶ *A crowd at Stone Mountain in Georgia enjoys a laser light show. The light plays across a carving in the mountainside. The brilliant beams of colored laser light reflect off mirrors and are projected onto the carving. They trace a series of fixed images so fast that the images appear to move like characters in a cartoon.*

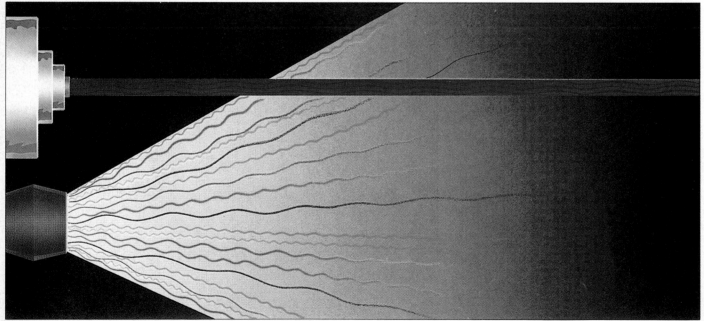

STEPHEN R. WAGNER

▲ *Compare the narrow beam of laser light, at the top, with the spreading beam of a flashlight. The wiggly lines in both represent light waves—the form in which light travels. The flashlight's waves have many colors because ordinary light, though it appears white, is really a mix of many different colored light waves. Each color has a different **wavelength,** measured between one crest, or peak, of a wave and the next. The light of a flashlight is **incoherent.** Its mixed waves spread out and become less bright. A laser light shoots straight out with a single bright color because its wavelengths are **coherent,** or organized.*

In the Looking Glass

As you brush your teeth, you look into the mirror. Of course, you see yourself. Light waves scattering off every part of your face strike the smooth, silvery mirror and reflect back to your eyes.

Light waves reflect off a mirror much as a ball bounces off a wall. Throw a ball straight at a wall and it bounces straight back to you. Throw the ball at an angle to the wall and the ball bounces away from you at an equal angle.

If you shine a flashlight straight at a mirror, its light reflects directly back at you. Tilt the beam and it bounces away. Physicists call a line straight out from the mirror a **normal** line. If you tilt the light, the angle between the light beam and the normal is the **angle of incidence.** The angle between the normal and the reflecting beam is the **angle of reflection.** The **law of reflection** states: The angle of incidence equals the angle of reflection.

▶ *How many young museum visitors do you see here? The visitors entered a three-sided room at the Exploratorium, in San Francisco. The walls are mirrors. With the visitors inside, the room turns into a giant kaleidoscope. Light that reflects off each child travels to a mirror. There it reflects onto a second mirror, from there onto a third mirror, and so on, until the eight children (Were you right?) look like quite a crowd. The eight visitors are shown in miniature at the right, without any of their reflections.*

Try it! Make a miniature kaleidoscope room. Buy three pocket mirrors at a drugstore. With rubber bands, strap them into the form of a triangle, each facing inward. Hold the triangle at eye level and slowly insert the eraser end of a pencil into it. The pencil will be reflected again and again. Move the pencil around, testing until you get the greatest number of reflections.

LOEL BARR

Catching the Rays

For centuries, people have used wood fires for heating and cooking. Over time, they have found other forms of fuel—coal, oil, gas, uranium, the sun—and new ways of using them.

How do people today capture the sun's heat to use it? One method is to let sunlight shine on dark panels with water in them. After the water heats up, pipes circulate it in the home to heat air.

Producing *electricity* from the sun's energy is more complicated. It involves the use of **photovoltaic** (fo-to-vahl-TAY-ik) **cells,** or solar cells. In a photovoltaic cell, the sun's energy moves **electrons** to produce electric current. Electrons are extremely tiny particles that exist in all matter. Electric current is made up of a stream of electrons.

▼ *Rays of sunlight allow 11-year-old Mary Jo Benjamin, of Great Barrington, Massachusetts, to listen to a solar-powered music box. When sunlight strikes the three pie-shaped* **solar cells,** *energy in the light causes atoms—very tiny parts of the cells— to release charged particles called* **electrons.** *Flowing electrons make an electric current. The current flows through a wire to a motor that turns a spool. Prickly spines on the spool pluck metal reeds that vibrate, sending music to Mary Jo's ears.*

▲ *Visitors twirl on a whirling ride in Los Angeles, California. The ride feels normal, but it's no ordinary one. It runs on sunshine. Panels beside the cars contain hundreds of* **photovoltaic cells.** *The cells convert sunlight to electricity and power the ride.*

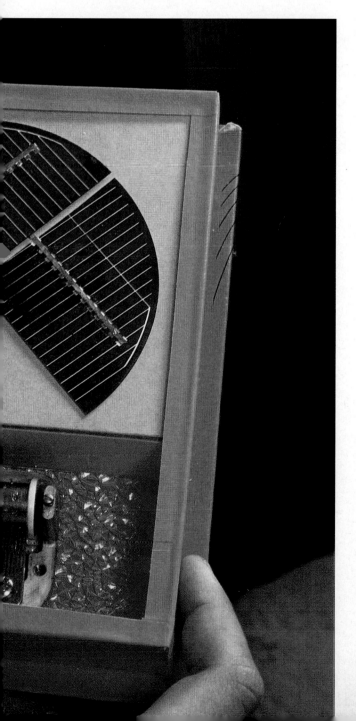

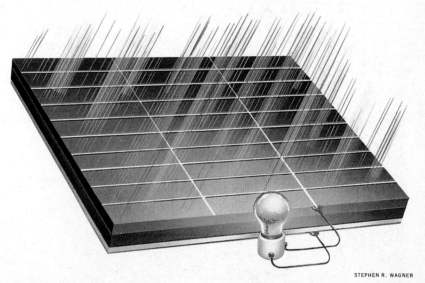

▲ *A photovoltaic cell is made with two thin layers of different kinds of silicon, the main substance in sand. They are shown in blue. Sunlight knocks electrons from the lower silicon layer to the upper layer, where they are trapped. A metal grid on top collects the electrons. From there, the electrons flow, as electricity, through a wire to a light bulb or other electrical appliance. The current returns to the cell through another wire.*

Physics Fun

Bubbles, Bubbles

Things you will need:
1 Cup of water
1 Cup of liquid detergent
1 Cup of glycerine (Buy it at a drugstore.)
  Large cake pan or cookie sheet
  Coat hanger or stiff wire

What to do:
Mix the water, detergent, and glycerine in a jar. Pour the mixture into the pan or cookie sheet. Bend the wire so that it forms a closed shape—a loop, a square, or a circle—with a handle. This is your bubble frame. Dip the frame into the bubble mix and slowly pull it out at an angle, so a film of liquid stretches across it. Wave the wire through the air and then give your wrist a flick to set free a giant bubble. *(Do this activity outdoors where bursting bubbles won't leave a mess.)*

Physics at work:
A water bubble without soap in it lasts only for a fraction of a second. A soap bubble lasts much longer. There's more to a soap bubble than you might think. A soap bubble is a bubble of water with soap concentrated on the inside and outside surfaces. The soap molecules reduce the normal surface tension of the water—the tendency of water to pull itself together. This allows the water molecules to stretch apart enough to form a longer-lasting bubble. With the glycerine, the soap on the inside and outside surfaces of a bubble also helps keep the water in the bubble from evaporating—and bursting the bubble.

At the Water's Edge

Things you will need:
  Eyedropper
  Large glass of water, filled to the brim
  Smaller glass of water

What to do:
Fill the eyedropper from the smaller glass. Use it to add water, one drop at a time, to the large glass. Even after the large glass looks full, you should be able to add many more drops. As you add water, watch it rise over the top but not overflow.

Physics at work:
Surface tension forms a tight "skin" over the top surface of the water. As you keep adding water, the skin stretches, just like the surface of a water balloon. But surface tension isn't *that* strong. If you add too much water, the skin will break.

Egg Float

Things you will need:
1 Fresh egg, cooked or uncooked
  Glass of water, almost full
  Teaspoon
  Salt

What to do:
Gently put the egg into the almost-full glass of water. The egg sinks, right? Now pour in two heaping teaspoons of salt and stir it around the egg. Does anything happen to the egg? Pour in two more teaspoons of salt. What happens? Add salt until the egg changes its location in the glass.

Physics at work:
The egg sinks at first because it weighs more than the fresh water it displaces. However, salt water is heavier than fresh water. When the water becomes salty enough, the salt water displaced by the egg weighs more than the egg—and the egg floats to the top.

LOEL BARR

What's the difference between music and noise? Noise is unorganized sound. Music is organized sound that can be pleasing to the ear. You make music by causing part of an instrument—or the air inside it—to vibrate. This creates rhythmic disturbances in the air that pulse outward to the ears of your audience. There are three main types of musical instruments. You pluck, bow, or strike strings on a stringed instrument, such as a guitar, a violin, or a piano. You vibrate a column of air in a wind instrument, such as a clarinet or a trumpet. You beat, shake, scrape, or smack together parts of a percussion instrument, such as a drum. Follow the directions on these two pages for a homemade orchestra. Can you make . . . *music?*

Ear, Hear!

What you will need:
  Rubber band

What to do:
Cut the rubber band in one place. Pull a section of it tight between your fingers and pluck it with your middle finger. It doesn't exactly produce a catchy tune, does it? Now hold the rubber band so that one end of it is near your ear. Pluck again. It's probably still not a catchy tune, but it should sound like music. Experiment with the tightness of the rubber band and see if you can produce different tones. Can you play a tune on the rubber band?

Physics at work:
A stretched rubber band vibrates, producing sound waves. Change the tension, or tightness, of the band, and you change the pitch. Pitch is determined by the number of times an object vibrates in a second. A tight band or string vibrates more rapidly than a loose one, and it produces a higher pitch, or sound.

Music Box

Things you will need:
  Empty cereal box
1 or 2 Thin wooden rods, plywood slats, or rulers
  4 Rubber bands

What to do:
Stretch the rubber bands around the box. Slip the wood or rulers under the rubber bands to lift the bands off the box. Pluck away! Slide the wood or rulers along the box to change the pitch, or the tones, of the instrument. Is your musical box louder and richer sounding than the rubber band you plucked at your ear?

Physics at work:
When the bands vibrate against the box, the box itself begins to vibrate. The vibrating box then causes more air to vibrate, creating a stronger sound. This same principle, by which a box or a sounding board increases loudness, is the basis for the sounds from guitars, pianos, violins, and other stringed instruments.

LOEL BARR

Jingle Nails

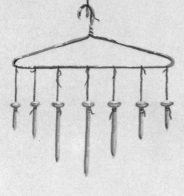

Things you will need:
8 Different-size nails made of the same material
Coat hanger
A few feet of thread or thin string

What to do:
Tie equal-length strings or threads to seven nails at their heads. Now tie the nails to the coat hanger. Dangle the hanger clear of any objects. Tap the nails with the extra nail to make music.

Physics at work:
Your nail chimes are an idiophone—a type of percussion instrument that naturally produces sounds when struck. Other idiophones include bells and cymbals.

Bottle Band

Things you will need:
Identical narrow-necked bottles (4 or more)
Water

What to do:
Fill the bottles with different amounts of water. Put your lower lip against the mouth of a bottle. Blow across the opening. Change the position of your lips until you hear a tone. Blow across each bottle in turn. By changing the water levels, you can change the pitch—how high or low the sound is.

Physics at work:
A bottle partly filled with liquid contains air at the top. When you blow across the top of the bottle, you vibrate the air inside, making sound waves. The pitch of the tone depends upon how fast the air vibrates. Vibrations will be slow for a tall volume of air and will sound low. Vibrations will be fast for a short volume of air and will sound high.

Going With the Beat

Things you will need:
2 Wooden spoons
Large coffee can
Large rubber band
Pinch of salt, sugar, or sand
Plastic wrap to cover the bowl

What to do:
Stretch the sheet of plastic wrap over the top of the can. Slip the rubber band around the sheet to keep it in place. Drop the salt, sugar, or sand onto the sheet. Now lightly drum away. Use the handles of the spoons as drumsticks. What do the little particles do when you beat your drum?

Physics at work:
The particles jiggle on top of the drum because the drumhead vibrates when you beat it. The vibrations of your homemade drum also set the air vibrating. This creates the sounds you hear.

2

PHYSICS
of
NATURE

A frog is a powerful leaper. Have you ever tried to touch one? The slippery creature probably spurted forward out of your reach. Some kinds of frogs can leap as far as 20 times their body length.

Muscular hind legs launch a frog into the air. Once off the ground, the frog continues to hurtle upward and forward. Then gravity slowly pulls it down while it continues to move forward. If you could trace the trajectory, or path, of the frog's leap, you would trace a graceful curve. Launch any weighty object that can't fly on its own and it will sail up, forward, and down in this same path. (A very light object, such as a feather, will be so affected by wind resistance that it won't follow this path.) The curve is called a **parabolic** (par-uh-BAHL-ik) **arc.**

Just as physics predicts that a frog's trajectory will draw a parabolic arc, so physics predicts and explains just about everything else that happens in the natural world around you: thunder, lightning, rainbows, sunsets, and even bats finding their way in the dark. The next few pages introduce the physical principles behind some of these things you might see occurring in nature.

Up, Over, and Down

A volcanic cinder, a frog, and *you* have something in common. Each tends to keep moving, once under way. If you doubt that, think of yourself on a bus. The driver hits the brakes. The bus lurches to a stop, but you don't. You bump the seat ahead of you.

You didn't stop moving when the bus did because of **inertia** (in-ER-shuh). The bus brakes acted on the bus, but they didn't act on you. Inertia kept you moving until the seat in front of you applied a force and stopped you.

All objects have inertia. It's a physical property that keeps moving things moving or keeps motionless things still—unless an outside force acts on them. Inertia kept you moving inside the bus until the force of the seat in front of you stopped you. A stationary object, such as a pebble resting on the ground, will continue to rest there motionless unless an outside force, such as your shoe kicking it, moves it.

Inertia tends to keep projectiles moving after they're launched. In space, far from any planet's atmosphere and gravity, a projectile just keeps going in a straight line. On earth, air friction slows down a projectile, and gravity pulls it down to the ground.

A frog leaps and will soon land on the next lily pad. If there were no force of gravity pulling the frog down, the creature would shoot off in the straight path shown by the red dotted line. That's what physicist Isaac Newton's first law of motion says: An object in motion will continue in motion in a straight line unless acted upon by an outside force. On earth, the force of gravity affects the path of the frog. So, instead of following a straight line, the frog curves back toward the ground, pulled by gravity. Its path is a parabolic arc. Gravity affects the frog's up-and-down motion, but not its forward motion. This drawing shows that, at any time, the frog has proceeded as far forward as it would have if it had continued in a straight line.

*The force of hot gases within the earth heaves up rocks and cinders in a volcano in Indonesia, a nation in southeastern Asia. The objects trace fiery curves in the shape of **parabolic arcs**. Objects launched into the air that cannot fly on their own follow parabolic arcs. Such objects are called **projectiles**. If you throw a rock or a baseball, the rock or ball becomes a projectile.*

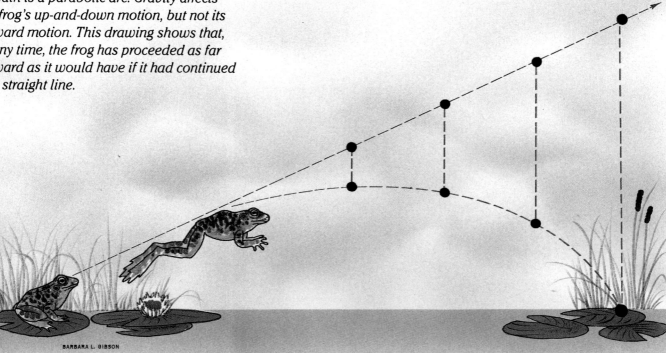

It's winter. You shuffle across a rug, touch a metal doorknob, and *zap!* You get an electric shock. Why? The molecules of the rug and of your feet are made up of smaller units called **atoms.** Electrons whiz around the center of each atom. Electrons have a negative charge. In the atom's center, particles called protons have a positive charge. The positive and negative charges usually cancel each other out, making an atom neutral. But an atom can pick up an extra electron and become negatively charged.

When you scuff your feet on a rug, electrons from the rug rub off onto you. You become negatively charged. If you touch metal, which conducts electrons well, the electrons will leap into the metal. The energy transfer gives you a tiny electric shock.

Electricity that builds up in this way is **static electricity.** It builds up in clouds because of friction between the air and ice or water droplets. When enough static electricity builds up, the electrons zigzag as lightning between the clouds or to the ground. This gigantic pulse of electric energy wallops the air—*kaboom!*—sending out huge sound waves, called thunder.

▶ *The lightning bolt flashing near farmhouses in Austria consists of the same kind of power that fuels your reading lamp: electricity. Electricity is a stream of electrons that give off energy as light and heat. In lightning, electrons flash between clouds or from a cloud to the ground. The heat of lightning sometimes starts fires.*

▶ *Why does a balloon that has been rubbed on clothing make a cat's hair stand on end? When you rub the balloon on cloth, the balloon picks up electrons. They give the balloon a negative electric charge. When you hold the balloon near hair, the negative charge repels, or pushes away, some of the negative charge in the hair. This leaves the hair positively charged. Positive and negative charges attract, so the hair rises toward the balloon. Tiny crackles you may hear are sparks caused by* **static electricity.**

Big Bolt With a Jolt

ROGER RESSMEYER

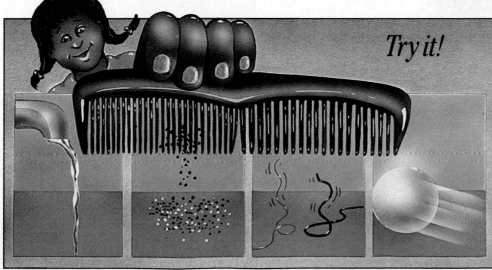

Try it!

Give a comb a negative electric charge by rubbing it against fur, silk, nylon, or wool. Hold it near some objects that move easily, and see what it will attract. Try a trickle of water from a faucet, salt and pepper, threads, a table-tennis ball, scraps of paper, your hair, or anything else that strikes your fancy.

LOEL BARR

Hot, liquid metal moves around deep inside the earth, along with the melted rock and minerals that form the earth's core. Many scientists believe that the movement of the liquid metal creates the **magnetic field** around the earth. Electrons spinning around the atoms of the hot metal produce a magnetic force.

Every electron in every substance pulls like a tiny magnet. In most substances, electrons spin in opposite directions from each other, which cancels out their magnetism. That's why most materials don't act as magnets.

But in some substances, the outer electrons may spin in the same direction. The combined magnetic power of those electrons produces a magnetic field, and that substance acts as a magnet. Only the metals iron, nickel, and cobalt—or other metals with those mixed in—can act as magnets. And only those metals will attract magnets. You can check that by trying to attach a magnet to an aluminum can or pot. Did it stick?

◄ *An eerie, flickering glow called the **aurora borealis** lights up the northern sky. These curtains of light, sometimes called the northern lights, are caused by electrically charged atomic particles from the sun. Normally, an area around the earth called the **magnetic field** traps these particles. But several times a year storms on the sun bombard the planets with them. The particles follow the magnetic field and enter the earth's atmosphere near the North and South Poles, causing a glow. These lights normally appear only in the far northern and southern parts of the planet. In the south, they are called the **aurora australis.***

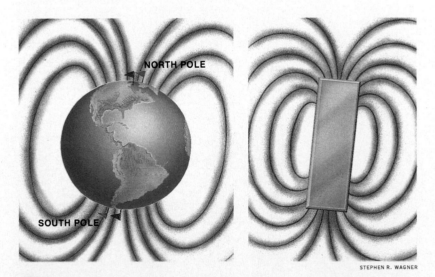

NORTH POLE

SOUTH POLE

STEPHEN R. WAGNER

▲ *The earth has a magnetic field, left, shown in orange, just like that of a bar magnet, right. Magnetic fields form in the patterns shown, but they are invisible. They curve between one magnetic pole and the other. The invisible fields are strongest near the magnetic poles. The earth's North Pole and South Pole, shown by blue flags, are near the magnetic poles, shown by red flags.*

'Attractive' Planet

▲ *Inside her compass, Christina Wong, 9, of San Francisco, has a magnetized needle. It shows her which direction she faces. The needle responds to the magnetic field of the earth. The ends of the earth's magnetic field, near the North and South Poles, are called the **magnetic poles.** The same end of a compass needle always points to the magnetic pole in the north.*

Quick Clicks for Catching Meals

Have you ever stood on a corner and listened to an approaching fire truck? You could almost certainly close your eyes and tell approximately where the fire truck was, in which direction it was moving, and how fast. Your ears would tell you.

To get the same kind of information, bats don't just listen to sounds that other things make. They make their own sounds and listen to the echoes. Bats, which have much better hearing than you have, rely on their ears to find their way—and their food.

A bat sends out sounds so high pitched that a human can't hear them. Detecting the echoes that return, the bat can judge the distance, speed, shape, path, size, and even the texture of an object no wider than a human hair. Some bats can pinpoint a motionless moth—a future meal—that's lying flat against a log.

Bat sounds are called ultrasound. Dolphins use ultrasound to navigate. Sailors use machine-made ultrasound to scan the ocean floor. Doctors use it to detect problems inside patients.

*As red bats hunt for insects at night, they use a system called **echolocation** (ek-oh-low-KAY-shun). Each bat makes rapid clicking sounds in its throat. The sound waves hit obstacles in the bat's path and bounce back to the bat's sensitive ears. The direction and timing of the echoes tell the bat exactly where the obstacle is.*

Try it!

Clear away objects between you and a large brick wall. Stand 20 steps back from the wall. Close your eyes, clap your hands, and listen for an echo. Take a step toward the wall and clap again. Repeat this many times. Do the echoes become louder and return to your ear faster as you approach the wall? Can you use sound to judge your distance from it?

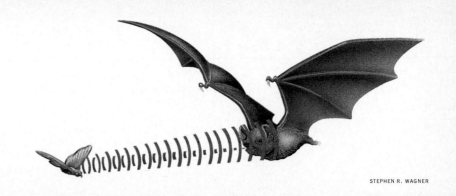

To find and catch an insect in the air, a bat first sends out its usual, obstacle-detecting clicks. When it finds a small flying obstacle, the bat starts clicking faster. It beams a narrow stream of sound waves, shown in blue, straight at the insect. Homing in on the source of the echoes, which are shown in orange, the bat snatches and swallows its prey.

STEPHEN R. WAGNER

Step outside after a rain. If you're lucky, a delicate, multicolored arc will appear across the sky. That rainbow demonstrates what physicist Isaac Newton discovered in 1666—that ordinary white light consists of a blend of lights of different colors.

To make a rainbow, rays of sunlight cross the sky above your head and strike a distant curtain of raindrops. Each ray enters a tiny, round drop. The ray bends slightly and fans out into its colors: red, orange, yellow, green, blue, and violet. This multicolored fan reflects off the inside of the raindrop and heads back toward you. As it leaves the drop, the fan of colors bends again and the colors spread out a little more. By the time the colors reach you, they are so spread out that you can see only one color from any one drop.

However, that isn't all it takes to make a rainbow. This process occurs in millions of raindrops at once. That's why you can see all the colors as you look at a rainbow.

Recipe for a Rainbow

Not one, but two, rainbows cross the sky over the Roaring Fork River, in Colorado. A rainbow appears when rays of sunlight enter millions of raindrops. Each drop causes the light to divide into the colors of the rainbow. Then the light reflects back to the viewer. When sunlight reflects <u>twice</u> inside each drop, a second rainbow appears. It's fainter because some light is lost in the second reflection. You'll notice that the colors of the second rainbow are reversed. That's because they were reflected an extra time. In the river, the light from both rainbows is reflected again.

*Glass **prisms** bend light, spread it out, and reflect it in the same way water drops do when they make rainbows. Here, strong beams of white light enter the prisms from the sides. Each beam bends and fans out into its separate colors. The colors reflect off the insides of the prisms, then bend again and fan out a little more as they leave the prisms. Each prism produces a bright, multicolored **spectrum,** or range of colors, that together form an <u>X</u>. In nature, each raindrop reflects only one of the separated colors directly at you, so it takes a great many raindrops to produce a rainbow.*

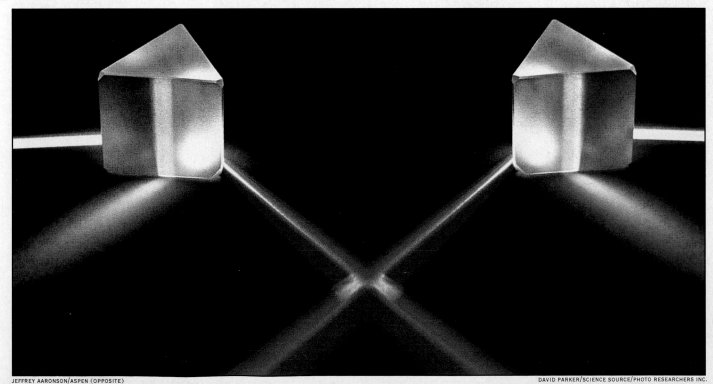

Built for Brightness

Imagine yourself lying in a blue hammock, watching the sunset. The sky grows darker and darker. Take a look at your hammock. It's not blue in the dark. The hammock turns black!

It might be hard to believe, but objects don't actually have colors of their own. They have qualities that *reflect* the colors found in the light that shines on them. That means that when there's no light, your hammock and all other objects have no color.

When light falls on the hammock, chemicals in the hammock called **pigments** absorb most of the colors in the light. But blue light is reflected to you, and the hammock appears blue. Pigment, or chemical color, is the most common basis for color. Most of the colors around you—the green in leaves, even your own skin coloring—are determined by pigments.

There's another kind of color, called **iridescence** (ir-uh-DES-ents). Iridescent color is caused by microscopic physical structures in objects, not by pigments. Iridescence produces purer, stronger color than pigment does, just as laser light is purer and stronger than ordinary light. The brilliant, shiny colors of peacocks and some butterflies are examples of iridescence.

How does iridescent color depend on microscopic structures? These layered structures in butterfly wings and in bird feathers reflect light waves so that some colors are canceled out and others are strengthened. On the iridescent butterfly at left, tiny ridges on its scales cancel most colors. Blue is reflected and strengthened. The blue is reflected only at certain angles, however. Change the angle of the light, and the blue turns to violet to muddy brown.

A peacock's colors don't depend on the angle of the light. Its structures are positioned so that only certain wavelengths can ever be reflected. A peacock isn't always shiny blue and green, however. Can you guess when it is not? In the dark, of course!

Millions of microscopic scales on the wings of a swallowtail butterfly are structured so that they reflect light—but only blue light. A shiny color created by reflected light is called **iridescence.**

The brilliant blues and greens in the tail of a peacock shimmer. Why? The peacock's colors come from light reflecting off tiny, shiny, layered scales in each feather. This iridescent color is brighter than the normal coloration of most other birds.

A bubble's iridescent colors come from light rays reflecting off both the inner and outer surfaces of the bubble. The two sets of reflections combine in different ways, depending on the angle of reflection and the thickness of the soap-and-water film that forms the bubble. Reflections combine and produce strong colors or they cancel each other out and produce no color.

The Color
Above You

If you've ever wondered why a sky that appears blue all day appears red or pink at sunrise and sunset, read on.

The earth's atmosphere forms a blanket of air that becomes thinner and thinner with increasing height. At altitudes of about 10 miles (16 km) and below, billions and billions of particles too small to see float in the atmosphere. When sunlight hits them, its different colors bounce off the particles and **scatter.** Blue and violet scatter the most. Orange and red scatter the least.

When the sun is overhead, its rays pass through the least amount of atmosphere. As you stand on the earth, the sky appears blue because blue light scatters the most. When the sun is low in the sky, at sunrise and sunset, its rays travel through a much thicker part of the atmosphere than at midday. By the time the morning or evening rays reach you, most of the blue has scattered out of them. The red is what's left to color the sky.

In 1883, an Indonesian volcano named Krakatoa erupted, blasting volcanic dust 17 miles (27 km) into the air. The eruption was 18 times bigger than that of Mount St. Helens in 1980. Carried by winds, Krakatoa's dust filled the atmosphere. The thick dust, filtering out blue light, caused brilliant sunsets worldwide.

▶ *Viewing the distant planet earth from the moon, you can see that the moon's "sky" appears black, even in daylight. That's because the moon has no atmosphere, and therefore no atmospheric particles to scatter sunlight. The clear, airless surroundings allow you to see deep into the blackness of space.*

◀ *Why is the sky blue, as it is over this lake in Colorado? When the short wavelengths of sunlight—violet and blue—hit tiny particles in the air, those colors bounce and spread. Blue skies are due to this **scattering.** Longer wavelengths—other colors—pass by the tiny particles.*

▼ *It's midmorning in Yakima, Washington, on May 18, 1980. Ash from the eruption of Mount St. Helens has darkened the sky, and streetlights are back on again. The thick, dense layer of volcanic ash particles in the sky has scattered blue light completely, allowing only sunset-colored light to reach the earth.*

Physics Fun

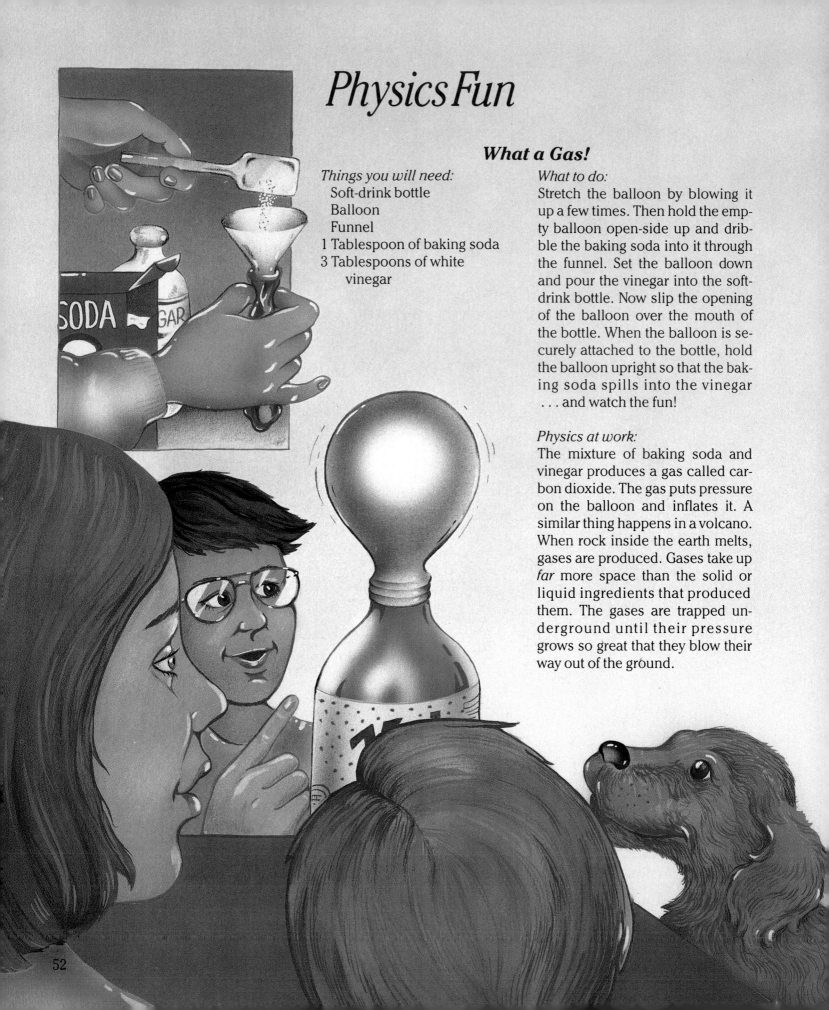

What a Gas!

Things you will need:
- Soft-drink bottle
- Balloon
- Funnel
- 1 Tablespoon of baking soda
- 3 Tablespoons of white vinegar

What to do:
Stretch the balloon by blowing it up a few times. Then hold the empty balloon open-side up and dribble the baking soda into it through the funnel. Set the balloon down and pour the vinegar into the soft-drink bottle. Now slip the opening of the balloon over the mouth of the bottle. When the balloon is securely attached to the bottle, hold the balloon upright so that the baking soda spills into the vinegar . . . and watch the fun!

Physics at work:
The mixture of baking soda and vinegar produces a gas called carbon dioxide. The gas puts pressure on the balloon and inflates it. A similar thing happens in a volcano. When rock inside the earth melts, gases are produced. Gases take up *far* more space than the solid or liquid ingredients that produced them. The gases are trapped underground until their pressure grows so great that they blow their way out of the ground.

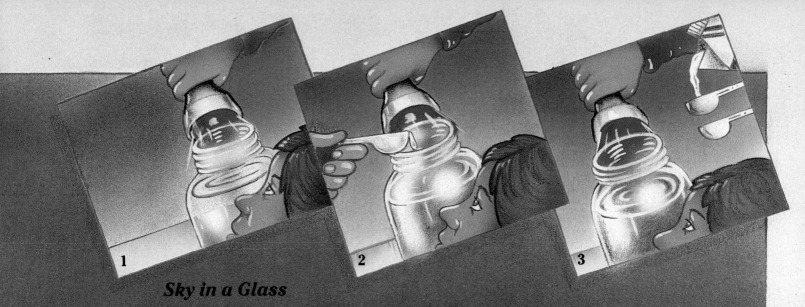

Sky in a Glass

Things you will need:

Clear jar of fresh water   1/4 Cup of milk
Flashlight   Tablespoon

What to do:
1. Shine the light through the clear water from the back of the jar. Does the water have any color? **2.** Stir a tablespoon of milk into the water. Shine the flashlight the same way again. Do you see any blue in the jar? **3.** Add another tablespoon of milk and shine the light again. Keep stirring in tablespoons of milk and shining the light until the fluid inside appears pink.

Physics at work:
When you shined the light through the clear water, you saw no color. That's the way the sky would look to you on the moon. The space above you would have no air and therefore no particles to scatter light. You'd see clearness (and the blackness of space, beyond). When you first added milk, blue wavelengths of light scattered off the particles of milk, as they do in the midday sky. When you added more milk, your "atmosphere" became thicker. It scattered the remaining red wavelengths, just as the real atmosphere does at dawn and at dusk.

North, South, East, West

Things you will need:

Needle   Tissue
Glass of water   Fork
Magnet

What to do:
First magnetize the needle. Stroke the needle with the magnet a hundred times, always in the same direction. This lines up groups of atoms in the needle so that their electrons spin in the same direction, creating a magnetic field. Tear off a stamp-size square of tissue. Lay it on the water and lay the needle on it. Gently poke the tissue with the fork until the tissue sinks. Surface tension should hold up the needle. Does the needle slowly swing around and point in one direction? Turn the glass carefully. Does the needle always tend to point in the same direction?

Physics at work:
You've made a compass. The needle lines up with the lines of magnetic force between the earth's north and south magnetic poles. If you know where north is, you'll know which end of your needle is the one pointing north.

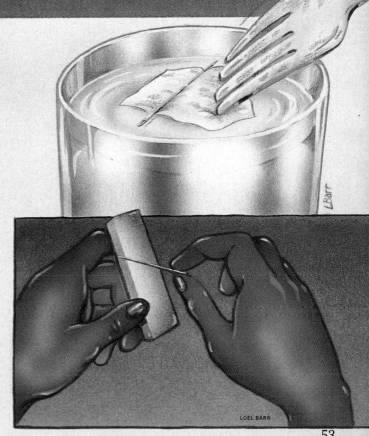

LOEL BARR

Homegrown Rainbow

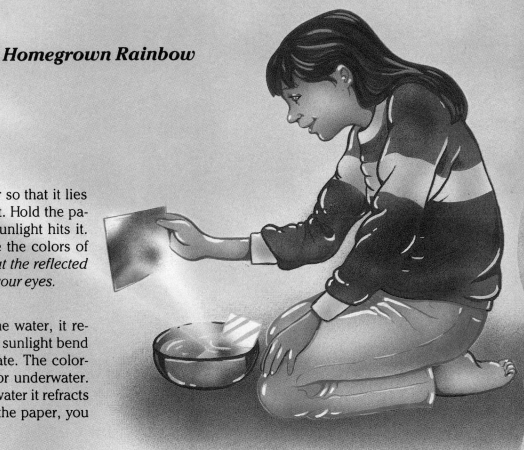

Things you will need:
- Bowl of fresh water
- Small mirror
- Piece of white paper
- Direct sunlight

What to do:
Prop up the mirror in the bowl of water so that it lies mostly underwater and reflects sunlight. Hold the paper above the mirror so the reflected sunlight hits it. Hold the paper steady. You should see the colors of the rainbow appear on it. *Do not look at the reflected sunlight in the mirror. It could damage your eyes.*

Physics at work:
As sunlight passes from the air into the water, it refracts, or bends. The different colors in sunlight bend different amounts, so the colors separate. The colorful, refracted light reflects off the mirror underwater. As the reflected light passes out of the water it refracts a little more. When the reflection hits the paper, you should see the colors of the rainbow.

Feather Light

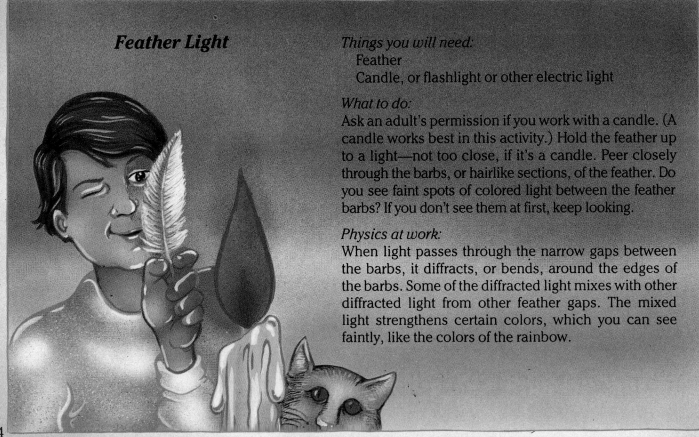

Things you will need:
- Feather
- Candle, or flashlight or other electric light

What to do:
Ask an adult's permission if you work with a candle. (A candle works best in this activity.) Hold the feather up to a light—not too close, if it's a candle. Peer closely through the barbs, or hairlike sections, of the feather. Do you see faint spots of colored light between the feather barbs? If you don't see them at first, keep looking.

Physics at work:
When light passes through the narrow gaps between the barbs, it diffracts, or bends, around the edges of the barbs. Some of the diffracted light mixes with other diffracted light from other feather gaps. The mixed light strengthens certain colors, which you can see faintly, like the colors of the rainbow.

LOEL BARR

Homemade Thunder

Things you will need:
  Sheet of ordinary paper
    8 inches (20 cm) square
  Sheet of heavy paper 8 inches
    (20 cm) square (called a
    card, below)
  Ruler
  Pencil
  Scissors
  Transparent tape

What to do:
1. Draw a line along one edge of the ordinary paper, ½ inch (1½ cm) in from the edge. Do the same along an adjoining edge.

3. Place the card over the paper, up against the two pencil lines. Fold the edges of the paper up and over the card.

2. Using the ruler, draw a straight line diagonally across the paper, making sure both lines you have already drawn lie on the same side of the diagonal. Cut along the diagonal line, and throw away the half without the lines on it.

4. Tape down the edges of the folded paper securely onto the card.

6. Now hold the untaped corner of the card. Swing your arm down and snap your wrist—fast!

5. Turn the card and paper over. Fold the card in half, as shown.

Physics at work:
As the paper snaps out of the card, it smacks the air in its path, causing the air to vibrate and make a loud crack. Lightning also causes air to vibrate by giving it a hard whack. This results in . . . thunder!

3

PHYSICS
at
HOME

With a furry friend nearby, Cathleen Padua, 8, of San Francisco, sends her hair flying with a jet of hot air. The hot air heats up the water that coats each wet hair. As the water molecules heat up, they start to jiggle faster—and farther apart—although they're so tiny you can't detect any movement. Soon, the fastest-moving molecules break away and rise into the air. They have changed from a liquid into a gas called **water vapor.** This change is called **evaporation.** When most of the water molecules on Cathleen's hair have evaporated, her hair will be just about dry.

When Cathleen first stepped out of the shower, water droplets fogged the mirror. Water vapor in the damp air had struck the glass and cooled off. The cooling process made the vapor molecules slow down and gather together, turning the vapor back to a liquid. This change is called **condensation.**

Changes from liquid to gas, and gas to liquid, are called changes in the state of matter. You witness matter changing states all the time, although you might not have thought about the changes that way. Can you think of examples you have seen at home? You'll find some in the pages of this chapter.

From State
to State

The change in state from a liquid mixture to solid vanilla ice cream is a tasty one. Not all changes in state are as delicious, but all follow the same basic rules. A change in state requires a transfer of energy, usually the addition or subtraction of heat.

How does heat travel? Dip a metal spoon into a steaming cup of hot chocolate. The heat from the liquid causes the molecules in the spoon to heat up and start to jiggle. They bump into the molecules next to them and start them jiggling, and so on all the way up the spoon. Soon, the heat reaches the end of the spoon and . . . Ouch! It's hot!

Because heat is easily conducted, or carried, through metal, metal is called a good heat **conductor.** Materials that don't conduct heat well, such as air and wood, are called **insulators.** The aluminum can in the ice-cream maker below conducts heat from the cream inside to the ice around it.

Heat always flows from a warmer object to a cooler one. When you put ice cubes into hot tea, you may think the ice cools off the tea. Actually, the tea melts the ice cubes—and the tea loses heat in the process. Eventually, the ice will melt away, consuming heat energy from the tea, and therefore leaving it cooler.

▲ *Ricardo Martinez, 10, Elizabeth Dong, 7 (center), and Vanessa Mendoza, 8, of San Francisco, combine physics and pleasure by changing liquid into one of the world's favorite solids—ice cream. Ricardo pours a mixture of milk, cream, sugar, eggs, and vanilla into a metal can inside the ice-cream maker. The girls will then pack crushed ice around the can. They will add salt to the ice. The salt helps melt the ice and make the meltwater bath colder than ice and water alone.*

▲ *Vanessa sets an electric motor in place. It will turn a paddle that makes sure the sweet mixture cools off evenly. The mixture, much warmer than the ice around it, transfers—and loses—its warmth to the ice.*

ROGER RESSMEYER (ALL)

It's time to sample the product. In half an hour, the mixture has transferred so much of its heat to the ice that the ice has melted and the mixture has frozen. The mixture changed state from a liquid to a solid.

59

Frozen condensed water vapor, which you probably know as frost, forms icy ferns on a windowpane. When water vapor in the air condenses at a freezing temperature, such as on a freezing window, it changes directly from a gas to a solid: ice. Physicists call this process **deposition.** *What makes a substance stiff when it's a solid, watery when it's a liquid, and airy when it's a gas? In a solid, strong bonds have developed between the molecules, pulling them into rigid structures called* **crystals.** *You can see the shapes of ice crystals in frost and in snowflakes. In liquids, molecules are tightly packed but bonds between them are weaker. Bonds between gas molecules are weakest.*

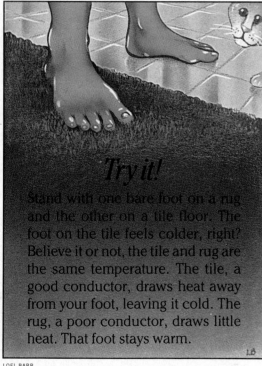

Try it!

Stand with one bare foot on a rug and the other on a tile floor. The foot on the tile feels colder, right? Believe it or not, the tile and rug are the same temperature. The tile, a good conductor, draws heat away from your foot, leaving it cold. The rug, a poor conductor, draws little heat. That foot stays warm.

Have you ever heard anyone use the expression "slower than molasses"? Perhaps someone has even said that about you as you walked really slowly on your way to school. Molasses *is* slow. Pour it and it just oozes along.

This slowness is caused by a kind of friction in liquid, called **viscosity** (viss-KAHS-uht-ee). Viscosity is caused by the molecules of a liquid rubbing together. Water has low viscosity. It pours easily. Honey and molasses have high viscosity. They ooze.

The viscosity of ordinary fluids can be changed by changing their temperature. Heat honey or many kinds of oil, and they will flow more easily. Chill them, and they will flow more slowly. Fluids that behave this way are called Newtonian fluids.

Other kinds of fluids, called **non-Newtonian fluids,** have their viscosity changed another way. You apply force—either a pull or a push. When you yank on Silly Putty®, a non-Newtonian fluid, its viscosity increases so much that it won't flow at all. Instead, it breaks. Other non-Newtonian fluids do the opposite. You apply force and their viscosity decreases. Margarine is one of these. It behaves like a solid, but push on it and you can spread it easily.

Ooze, Stretch, Snap, Shatter, and Pop

*Donald Hammonds, 7, of San Francisco, yanks a piece of Silly Putty®. Snap! It breaks. Like water and air, this putty is a fluid, but it's a weird kind of fluid. If you pull on it fast, it snaps. If you pull slowly, it stretches. Called a **non-Newtonian fluid,** the putty sometimes behaves like a solid, sometimes like a liquid.*

Donald pulls slowly and evenly on the soft putty, and it stretches. Follow the directions on page 74 and you can make a non-Newtonian fluid of your own. Few such fluids occur in nature. There is a naturally occurring one, however, that you've certainly heard about: quicksand.

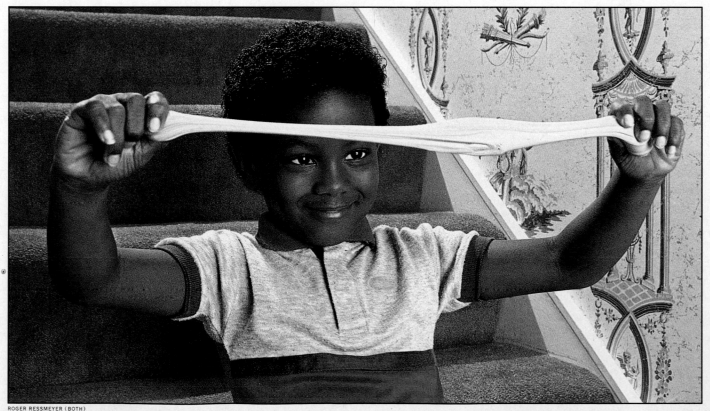

ROGER RESSMEYER (BOTH)

63

A World Under Pressure

You've probably heard the description "lighter than air." You may even have used the description yourself. Now, air may *seem* light, but like anything else, if you have enough of it, it becomes heavy. Standing at sea level, you've got miles and miles of air above you. Those miles of air add up so that a column of air pushes down on every square inch ($6\frac{1}{2}$ cm²) of your body with a weight of about 15 pounds (7 kg).

Why aren't you exhausted from carrying around the weight of the atmosphere? It's because the fluid pressure pushing out from inside your body exactly equals the **atmospheric pressure** pushing down on you.

Although the atmosphere extends hundreds of miles up, most of the air molecules lie near the earth, pulled there by gravity. Out of all the miles of atmosphere, 99 percent of the air occupies the lower 19 miles (30 km). Above that, air molecules are so spread out that the air is said to be "thin." Air actually begins to thin out not so far above sea level. Many mountain climbers and skiers become short of breath at an elevation of only 2 miles (3 km). On very high routes, most climbers carry oxygen tanks to provide the oxygen they need to breathe easily.

Try it!

Atmospheric pressure is powerful stuff. You can show that with newspaper, a hammer, and an arm's-length thin wooden slat or paint stirrer. Lay the wood on a work table with about a quarter of it over the edge. Smooth two sheets of newspaper over the part of the wood on the table. Now stand back and hit the end of the slat hard with a hammer. What happens? Atmospheric pressure on the paper holds down the paper—and the wood— causing the wood to snap in two.

▶ *Evan Card, 8, of San Carlos, California, drinks milk through an unusual straw, but it works like any other. The chances are that no straw works just the way you think it does. To bring milk to his mouth, Evan depends on **atmospheric pressure**, the pressure caused by the weight of the atmosphere. When Evan sucks on the straw, he reduces the atmospheric pressure in it. Then the normal atmospheric pressure, shown by the blue arrow, pushes down on the milk and forces it up through the straw and into Evan's mouth. The next time you drink through a straw, remember that your drink isn't <u>pulled</u> in by you. It's <u>pushed</u> in by atmospheric pressure.*

ROGER RESSMEYER

LOEL BARR

64

The Simplest Machine

If someone said, "Quick! Name a machine!" you might shout "Lawn mower!" You probably wouldn't cry "Lever!" People usually think of a machine as anything with a motor. Physicists, however, define a machine as anything that performs work. Work is done when something is moved by a force. A machine is a device used to move something else. A **lever** is one kind of machine. It consists of a bar that pivots on a fixed point. When you apply a force to one part of a lever, another part of it moves something. There are three kinds of levers. Compare them below and at right.

A machine can change the amount of force you apply in performing a job—either increasing the force or decreasing it. In using a lever, you make a trade. If you apply a small force over a long distance, the lever may apply a stronger force over a shorter distance. That's what happens when you pry open a paint can, as shown below. If you apply a strong force over a short distance, the lever may apply a weaker force—but over a longer distance. That's what happens with a broom, shown on the next page.

WILLIAM DEKAY

*Marissa Valeri, 9, of Wheaton, Maryland, uses a screwdriver to pry the lid off a paint can. The screwdriver becomes a **lever,** a kind of simple machine. A lever consists of a stiff bar that pivots, or turns, on a fixed point called the*

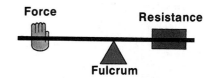

FIRST CLASS LEVER

Force

Resistance

Fulcrum

*fulcrum. Here, the fulcrum is the lip of the paint can. Marissa applies downward **force** on the screwdriver handle. The screwdriver pivots on the fulcrum and the tip of the screwdriver pops the lid up. The lid, the part that's being moved, provides **resistance.** A lever that has the fulcrum between the force and the resistance is called a first-class lever.*

When you use a nutcracker, you're using a second-class lever. The fulcrum is at the _end_ of the lever. You apply force at the other end. The resistance—a walnut—lies

SECOND CLASS LEVER

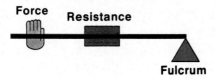

between the force and the fulcrum. Squeeze, and the lever pivots at the fulcrum and crushes the nut. You push down with a force and farther down the handle, the lever magnifies that force. What's another second-class lever? A wheelbarrow! The wheel is the fulcrum; the force is your hands; and the resistance is the load of dirt in between.

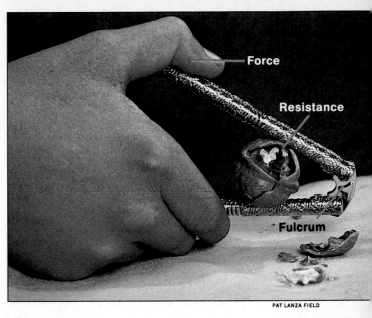

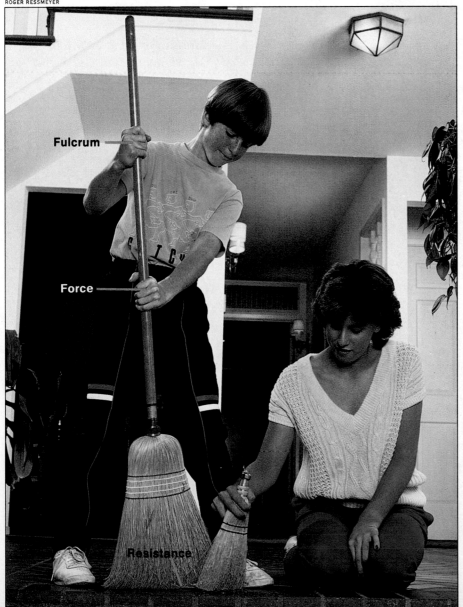

Michael Maguire, 11, and Ashley Card, 14, of San Carlos, sweep out the hall of Ashley's house. Did you recognize Michael's broom as

THIRD CLASS LEVER

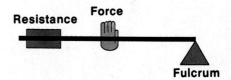

a lever? He holds his upper hand steady on the broom. That's the fulcrum. Farther down, his left hand applies force by pushing against the handle. The resistance—the friction between the floor and the broom straws—lies at the bottom of the broom. When you have a lever where the force lies between the resistance and the fulcrum, you have a third-class lever.

DIAGRAMS: BARBARA L. GIBSON

67

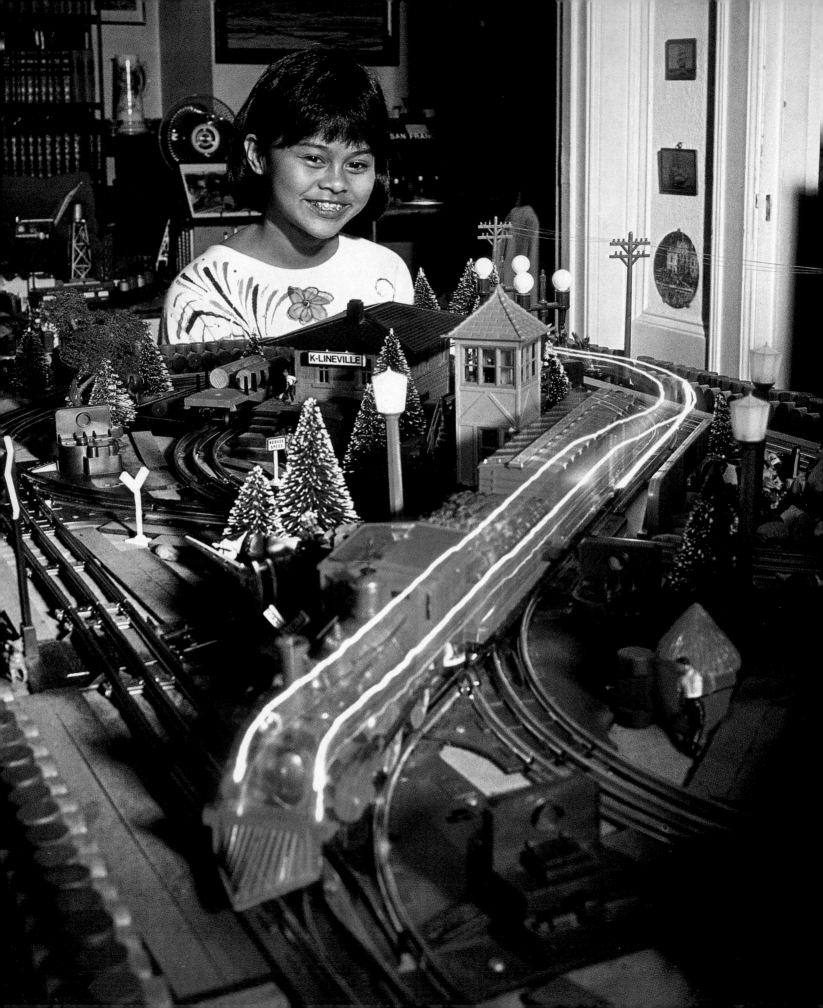

Many power line poles have large black boxes attached to them. Those boxes are **transformers,** like the transformer that controls the electric train Jennifer Padua runs, at left. Her transformer converts 120 volts from the wall socket to 8 volts for the train. It "steps down" the voltage. The large transformers on power lines also step down, or decrease, voltage. They reduce the high voltage coming in from the power company before it enters your house. The power company uses high voltage because high voltage loses less energy over distance than low voltage does.

Electric current comes in two forms: **direct current (dc)** and **alternating current (ac).** Direct current is the steady flow of electrons such as you get from a battery. Alternating current, which changes direction 60 times a second, is the form of electricity that runs into most North American homes. Ac can be transmitted more efficiently over distance than dc.

Taming Electricity

◄ *A specially exposed photograph captures movement as Jennifer Padua, 13, of San Francisco, runs an electric train. The train draws electricity from a wall outlet. But the outlet provides 120 volts—too much for the train motor and too dangerous for Jennifer in case she should get a shock. The voltage for the train is reduced by a **transformer.***

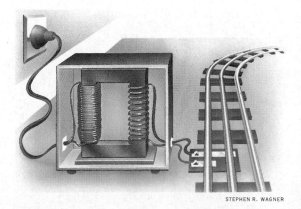

STEPHEN R. WAGNER

▲ *A transformer steps down, or reduces, the electrical voltage from the wall outlet. The wire from the wall, carrying 120 volts, loops many times inside the left part of the transformer in what's called the primary coil. The secondary coil, on the right, has far fewer loops. It picks up only a small part of the voltage from the primary coil and carries it out to the track. The secondary coil provides 8 volts—just enough for the train.*

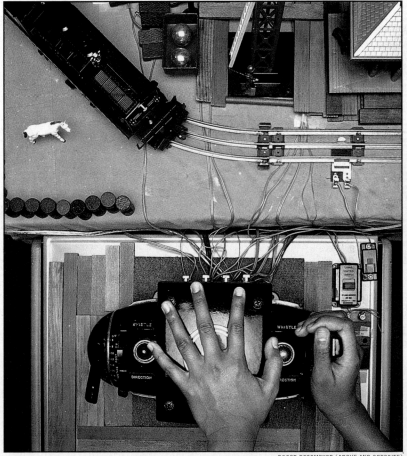

ROGER RESSMEYER (ABOVE AND OPPOSITE)

▲ *When Jennifer switches on the transformer, electricity flows into it carrying the full 120 volts from the wall outlet. But to run her train safely, she needs a <u>maximum</u> of 8 volts. Using the control arms on the sides of the transformer, she can vary the voltage output to the track—from 0 to 8 volts. Low voltage makes the train move slowly. High voltage speeds it up. The wires leading under the rails carry electricity to extra equipment around the tracks.*

69

The Visible and the Invisible

You're on a family outing and it's your turn to sit in the front seat. The sun shines through the windshield. Its rays brighten the inside of the car because visible light passes through glass. Your face is warm from the sun because infrared (in-fruh-RED) rays also pass through glass. You can't see these rays, but they provide heat. You won't get a sunburn, however. Ultraviolet rays, the invisible rays that cause sunburn, cannot travel through glass.

Light waves—those you can see and those you can't—are part of a much larger group of electromagnetic waves. The group is called the **electromagnetic spectrum.** It includes gamma rays, X rays, ultraviolet rays, visible light, infrared rays, microwaves, TV and radio waves, and electrical waves. In a vacuum, all these waves travel at the same speed—the speed of light—but they behave in different ways. Light waves cannot pass through wood, but radio waves can. X rays pass through most of your body, but your bones and teeth absorb them. Gamma rays can travel through almost anything.

▼ *The air all around you is full of different kinds of electromagnetic waves. They transfer energy from one place to another. A few of them you can see: light waves. Most you can't see, such as radio waves and X rays. All of these waves can travel at the speed of light. They differ from each other in wavelength and in frequency. They can vary in the amounts of energy they carry. Read below about different kinds of waves in the **electromagnetic spectrum.***

▶ *Stephanie Romas, 9, of Belmont, California, tunes in to her favorite radio station. She twists the dial, setting the receiver at the exact **frequency** she wants. Frequency is one characteristic of radio waves. It tells you how many waves pass a given spot in one second. Low frequency waves have long wavelengths. High frequency waves have short wavelengths. Each radio station in your area has its own frequency.*

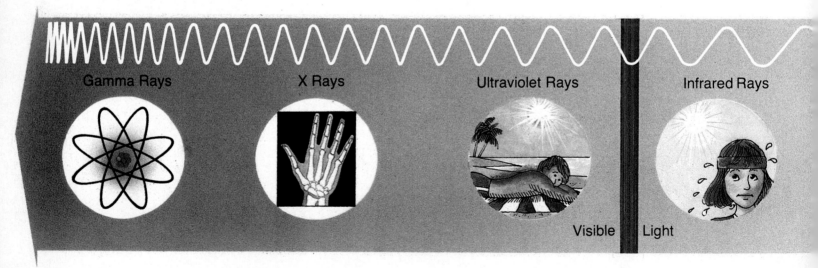

Gamma Rays   X Rays   Ultraviolet Rays   Infrared Rays

Visible   Light

*Waves with the shortest wavelength have the highest frequency. They also carry the most energy. These are **gamma rays,** given off by nuclear reactions in uranium and other radioactive substances. Gamma rays can go through lead and concrete and can be deadly. **X rays** fall next to gamma rays on the spectrum. You've probably had your teeth X-rayed. When the rays are beamed at your body, most of them pass through onto a photographic plate on the other side and darken it. Bones and teeth absorb X rays, leaving gray shadows on the plate that a doctor can examine. It's best to be exposed to X rays as little as possible. Overexposure can damage living cells. **Ultraviolet rays** are mostly absorbed by the atmosphere as they come from the sun, but some pass through to the ground. These rays cause sunburns. Ultraviolet light is invisible to humans. Most*

Microwaves

Radio Waves

insects, however, can see it. **Visible light,** including all the colors of the rainbow, comes next on the spectrum. You read about visible light in chapters 1 and 2. **Infrared rays** have slightly longer wavelengths than red light. You can't see them, but you can feel them. Often called radiant heat, these hot waves may be used to keep food warm and to dry hair. **Microwaves,** the shortest of radio waves, are used in microwave ovens to cook food, and in satellite communications. Satellites in space relay microwave messages between continents. Other **radio waves** cover a large portion of the electromagnetic spectrum. Different frequencies of radio waves are used for local television and for ship-to-shore radio. Among the longest waves of all are electrical waves that radiate from telephone wires carrying conversations.

Physics Fun

An Ice Idea

Things you will need:

Juice from 2 large lemons   2 Cups of sugar
Grated rind from 1 lemon   4 Cups of milk

What to do:

Combine the juice, rind, and sugar. Slowly stir in the milk. Pour this mixture into undivided ice cube trays or a small baking pan. Place the mixture in a freezer. Before the mixture has frozen completely, take it out and stir the sherbet to break up the large crystals. Return it to the freezer. When the mixture has frozen completely, enjoy it!

Physics at work:

In the freezer, heat flows from the sherbet mixture to the colder air. As the temperature of the mixture drops, the molecules in the mixture slow down and bond to each other in solid crystals. The mixture becomes a solid dessert.

An Ice Hot Idea

Things you will need:

2 Styrofoam cups   Hot tap water
  or unwaxed paper cups   Cold tap water

What to do:

Fill one cup with cold water. Then, being careful not to burn yourself, fill the other cup with very hot tap water. Put about the same amounts of water in each cup. Immediately place both cups in the freezer. Which will freeze first?

Physics at work:

The hot water should freeze first! Why? Both cups lose some heat through conduction to the freezer air. Both also lose some water through evaporation. But the hot water evaporates *much* faster. Evaporation involves a great loss of heat energy. As the hot water evaporates, its temperature drops rapidly—faster than that of the cold water. The hot water "catches up" to and "passes" the cold water, and freezes first.

72

LOEL BARR

Pick a Penny

Things you will need:
5 Pennies, each with a different date
  Plate
  Hat
  Group of friends

What to do:
Place the pennies on a plate. Ask a friend to pick out one penny and look at the date. Have the group pass it around until each person has checked the date. Promptly put all of the pennies into the hat and shake them up. Reach in without looking and surprise your friends by pulling out the one they had picked!

Physics at work:
Copper conducts heat easily. When the warm hands held the copper penny, the penny absorbed their heat. Feel around inside the hat for the warm penny, and .... *Abracadabra!* You'll find the right one!

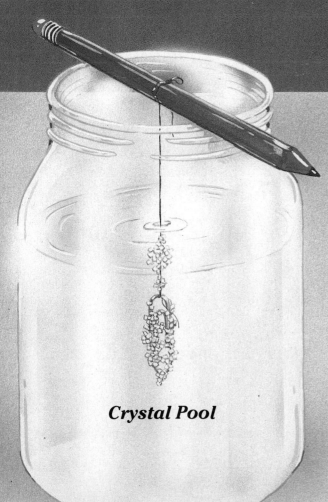

Crystal Pool

Things you will need:

1 Cup of water	Wooden spoon	Thread
2 Cups of sugar	Thick glass jar	Paper clip
Saucepan	Pencil or stick	

What to do:
Ask permission from an adult before using the stove. Pour the water into a saucepan and bring it to a boil. Reduce the heat. Slowly stir in the sugar, a little at a time, until no more will dissolve. Let the solution cool a bit, then pour it into the jar. Tie one end of the thread to the pencil and the other end to the paper clip. Wet the thread and the clip, and brush them through dry sugar until sugar crystals stick to them. Lower the paper clip gently into the solution. If the crystals fall off, pull out the thread and try again. (New crystals will take *weeks* to form unless you get a few sugar crystals to stick to the thread or paper clip at the start.) Let the pencil lie across the mouth of the jar. Watch sugar crystals form on the thread and the paper clip. It can take several days.

Physics at work:
Sugar dissolves in water. Much more dissolves in hot water than in cold water. As the temperature in the sugar water cools, the water cannot hold as much sugar in solution. Some of the sugar is forced to change from a liquid back to solid crystals.

Airlift

Things you will need:

    Glass of water   Index card

What to do:

Fill the glass about three-quarters of the way with water. Hold the card tightly over the top of the water glass with your palm, and turn the glass upside down. Gently let go of the card. Does the water gush out?

Physics at work:

The water should stay where it is in the overturned glass. When you turn the glass over, the water sloshes to the card, and some air is trapped above it. When you remove your hand from the card, the card bends ever so slightly from the weight of the water. The air space inside the glass stretches, reducing the air pressure. That means the atmospheric pressure below the card is now just a bit greater than the pressure of the air inside the glass. What happens? Atmospheric pressure from below holds the card and the water in place.

'Goo' With the Flow

Things you will need:

1 Cup of water	Large mixing bowl
1½ Cups of cornstarch	Tablespoon

What to do:

Pour the water into the bowl. Gradually stir in the cornstarch until the mixture is slightly thicker than heavy cream. As you stir, tap the surface with the spoon occasionally. Soon, the mixture will stir like a liquid, but you'll be able to hit it with the spoon without splattering it. What you'll have is a liquid that acts in some ways like a solid. Whack it, roll it into a ball, break it, spread it. Is it a liquid or a solid? *To dispose of your non-Newtonian fluid, pour it into a jar with a lid, or seal it in a plastic bag. Then throw it into the trash. Do not pour it down a drain or toilet. It will clog the plumbing.*

Physics at work:

You have made a non-Newtonian fluid. It has the qualities of both a liquid and a solid. In a liquid, the molecules move around loosely. In a solid, the molecules remain in a fixed position. In your homemade mixture, long chains of molecules coil around each other. They will not flow easily under high pressure or force.

Pick-up Clips

Things you will need:
    Nail, 3 inches (8 cm) long
    Insulated copper wire, 6 feet (2 m) long
2 D-size flashlight batteries

    Pocket knife
    Paper clips or loose staples
    Transparent tape or adhesive tape

What to do:

Wind the wire around and around the nail, leaving about 6 inches (15 cm) of wire at each end. Ask an adult to help in cutting the insulation off the last inch (2½ cm) of both ends of the wire. Stack the two batteries top to bottom, or lay them on their sides top to bottom. Hold or tape an end of the wire against each end of the stacked batteries while you use the wrapped nail to pick up paper clips. You can even try to pull the nail from the coiled wire and use the nail as a permanent magnet. You may wish to test your permanent magnet on objects around the house. See what effect your magnet has on the needle of a compass.

Physics at work:

You've made an electromagnet. When you connected the wire to the batteries, the batteries caused an electric current to flow through the wire. The current created a magnetic field inside the nail, and the nail became an electromagnet. If the magnetic field was strong enough, the nail retained some magnetism when you pulled it from the wire coil. Then it became a permanent magnet. A magnet should attract most metals in your home that contain iron, cobalt, or nickel. When you place your magnet close to a compass, it should attract the compass needle even more strongly than the earth's magnetic field does. The chances are that you were able to attract the compass needle so that it no longer pointed north.

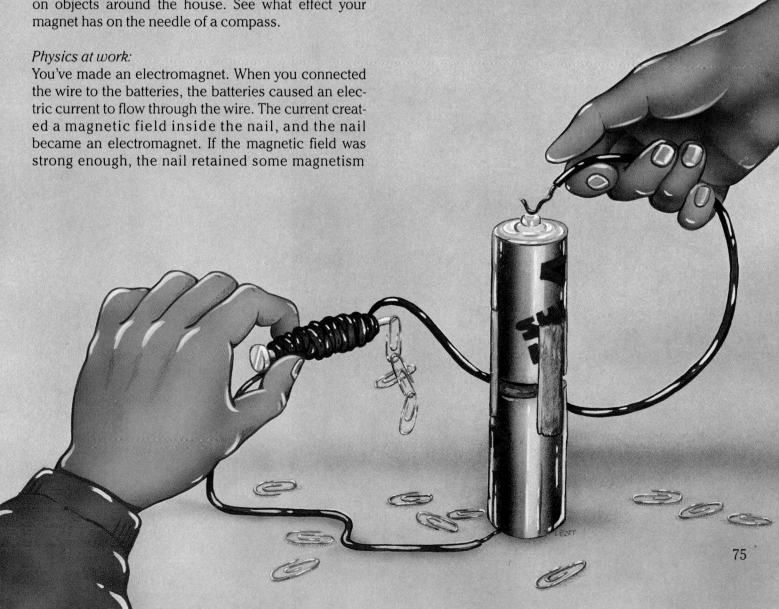

4

PHYSICS
of
SPORTS

In the 1968 Olympic Games, high jumper Dick Fosbury startled viewers by flopping headfirst and backward over the bar. This jump won Fosbury a gold medal and a place in history. His winning style, used by top high jumpers today, is called the Fosbury flop.

Why is the Fosbury flop such a winner? It has to do with a jumper's **center of gravity.** The center of gravity is the place where the entire weight of an object appears to be concentrated. Your center of gravity is usually behind your navel.

The center of gravity can actually be *outside* the body of an object. This may sound impossible, but take a doughnut as an example. Its center of gravity is in the center of the doughnut—in thin air.

Using the Fosbury flop, high jumper Sue McNeal, of Carlsbad, California (left), clears a bar. By curving her body into the shape of a half-doughnut, she moves her center of gravity down and *outside* her body. That's the secret of the Fosbury flop's success. Jumpers go higher than their centers of gravity, and clear higher bars. McNeal is one of many athletes who have winning ways with physics. In this chapter, discover how physics benefits other athletes.

Where the Center Goes

If you toss a baseball bat, chances are it will tumble end over end. If you photographed the bat's path, you'd see that it resembles the curve that Derwin Patterson follows (right). Both the bat and Patterson revolve around their **center of gravity**—and the center of gravity for each follows a **parabolic arc.**

An unevenly weighted object, such as the baseball bat, has its center of gravity near the heavier end. Try balancing a bat held sideways on your hand. When it balances, you'll know its center of gravity is nearer the thick end, directly above your hand.

The parabolic arc, which you read about in chapter 2 on page 38, appears in a great many sports. You yourself follow the path of a parabolic arc on many occasions. Every time you jump or dive, your center of gravity takes that curved path. Every time you toss a ball or heave a javelin or a stick, the thrown object follows a parabolic arc.

▶ *Captured on film seven times as he jumps, Derwin Patterson performs a "barani." Leaping from a small trampoline, he becomes a projectile and will shortly land on a mat. The yellow X's represent his **center of gravity.** The dashed line shows the curved path his center of gravity takes. Like the center of gravity of any projectile, Patterson's center of gravity traces a parabolic arc.*

BARBARA L. GIBSON

◀ *When this high jumper leaps, he raises his center of gravity as high as possible. On the left, he clears the bar using the straddle jump, the old position for high jumping. His center of gravity, inside his body, is marked by an X. On the right, using the Fosbury flop, he raises his center of gravity equally high. By arching his body, however, he himself goes <u>higher</u> than his center of gravity . . . and he clears a higher bar.*

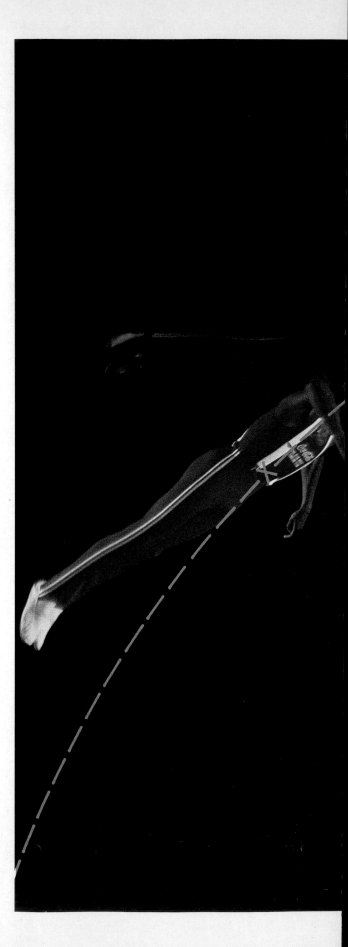

Gymnasts often find themselves in shaky positions. They have to line up their bodies precisely, in order to maintain their balance. They must place their **center of gravity** directly over a supporting base—their hands or feet. The wider the base, and the lower the center of gravity, the more stable the position is.

Have you ever watched professional football players take a position at the line of scrimmage? They squat with their feet planted far apart. Once the action starts, the players burst into motion, but they maintain that low, widespread stance. *Whammo!* Two players slam into each other in a block. Neither one of them, however, is knocked over. That's because their bases, the areas between their feet, are wide. By squatting down, they keep their centers of gravity low and their bodies stable.

You're an expert at managing your own balance, although you don't think about it much. Standing on a moving bus, don't you keep your feet far apart? That gives you a good chance of keeping your center of gravity over your feet. If you placed your feet close together, you'd fall over as soon as the bus lurched.

Balancing Act

Mary Lou Retton achieves perfect balance on a beam during the 1984 Olympic Games. To stay in competition, she had to line up her center of gravity directly over her supporting foot. That wasn't an Olympic requirement. It was a physics requirement. If she hadn't lined up her center of gravity correctly, she'd have toppled off the beam . . . and out of the running.

Try it!

Ask a friend to stand with his heels up against a wall. Place a ball at his feet and ask him to pick it up *without moving his feet*. He won't be able to. Why? When he bends over, his center of gravity shifts forward. To keep his balance, he would have to move his feet forward so that his base would shift, too.

LOEL BARR

Mary Lou does a handstand in a split position, sometimes called a walkover. The space between her hands provides the base for the pose. The gold medalist positions her center of gravity directly over her base, and balances there. It's a small base, a fact demanding that she balance delicately to stay up on the beam.

81

Human Levers at Play

Dwight Gooden is on the mound. The batter is in the box. Gripping the ball, Gooden winds up. He draws the whole right side of his body back. He keeps his left foot forward and his right foot back. Suddenly, he throws his weight forward. He whips his arm toward home plate and releases the ball. His arm works as a **lever** and magnifies the speed of the ball. The ball leaves his hand traveling about 90 miles an hour (145 km/h). It reaches the batter in less than half a second.

Imagine Gooden pitching that ball with his throwing arm tied to his side. The ball probably would, at best, roll slowly toward home plate. A pitcher's arm—and yours—is an effective lever. It allows you to magnify speed in many types of sports. In handball, your arm turns into a fast-swinging "bat." In swimming, each arm serves as a long, churning paddle in the water. In hockey and in baseball, you hold long pieces of equipment that act as extensions of your arms. These extra-long levers hurl pucks or bat balls at fantastic speeds.

Resistance

Force

Fulcrum

Resistance

Force

Fulcrum

Boris Becker, 18, of the Federal Republic of Germany, shows the serving style that helped him win the Wimbledon tennis tournament, in England. Boris's serving arm and his racket work together as a third-class lever. His shoulder acts as the **fulcrum,** *where his straight arm pivots. The muscles of his upper arm deliver the* **force.** *The* **resistance** *occurs where the ball hits his racket.*

STEVE POWELL/SPORTS ILLUSTRATED

Dwight Gooden, of the New York Mets, lets fly with his fast ball— which has been clocked as fast as 96 miles an hour (154 km/h). Like anyone else who throws, Gooden uses his arm as a third-class lever. At this point in the pitch, his forearm pivots at the elbow, which is the fulcrum. The muscles of his forearm supply the force, and the ball provides the resistance. The lever action of a pitch magnifies the speed a pitcher can give to the ball. (You can see another third-class lever in chapter 3 on page 67.)

Victory Around the Bend

Back in 1947, when Ulick O'Connor was the pole-vaulting champion of Ireland, pole-vaulters used bamboo poles. Bamboo didn't bend too well. It often snapped. "When the bamboo pole curved," says O'Connor, "it usually did not straighten out again. There would be a splintering sound as you flew through the air with half the pole in your hand."

Today, pole-vaulters use fiberglass poles. After bending, a fiberglass pole returns to its original shape. That's because it is made of **elastic** material. If you use force to change the shape of an elastic object, the object returns to its normal shape when the force is removed. That's what happens with a rubber band.

A pole-vaulter takes advantage of the elastic quality of the fiberglass pole. It gives the vaulter a big boost. The world record vault with a bamboo pole was 15 feet 7¾ inches (4¾ m). The fiberglass record is more than 4 feet (1¼ m) higher.

BARBARA L. GIBSON

A pole-vaulter uses a fiberglass pole to heave himself over a high bar. He sprints, plants the pole in a pit, and jumps up. He swings himself into a handstand as the bent pole springs back straight again. This springing action helps him over the bar.

2

1

*A remote-control camera below the high bar records this pole-vaulting sequence. Holding the pole over his head, Mike Tully, of Long Beach, California, runs toward the jump. **1.** He plants his pole and pushes off hard. Some of his kinetic, or moving, energy bends the pole. The kinetic energy is converted to a kind of potential energy called **elastic energy. 2.** Mike starts to swing his feet up. **3.** He rocks back, holding on upside down. As the pole springs back to its original shape, it*

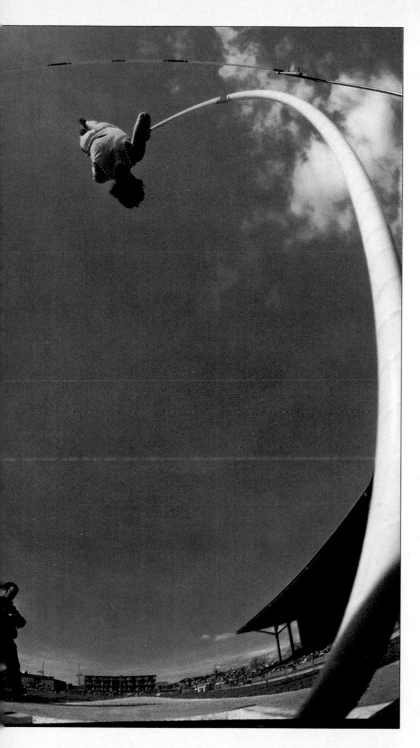

converts the elastic energy back to kinetic energy. This gives Mike an extra boost. **4.** He pushes himself off the pole, shoves it away from himself, and clears the bar. Did you heave a sigh of relief? Don't relax yet. Mike is still 18 feet ($5\frac{1}{2}$ m) above the ground. He still has to drop down to a safe landing in a padded pit.

Not All Are Round

The next time you step into a sporting-goods store, think for a second about why there are so many kinds of balls on display. Almost every sport requires its own kind of ball, and for good reason. Can you imagine playing volleyball with a basketball, or table tennis with a golf ball? How about bowling with a football? Each ball was designed with certain physical characteristics—weight, amount of material, elasticity, surface texture, shape, and size—that make it just right for its sport.

Foam Rubber Ball

So light that it has little inertia, this ball won't hurt people or break things when it hits them. The irregular surface of the spongy ball gives it plenty of friction and thus helps slow it down in the air. It's perfect for a rainy-day game indoors—but get permission to play with it in the house.

Tennis

A tennis ball is made of hollow rubber with a covering of wool-and-nylon felt. The rubber and compressed air inside make the ball elastic and bouncy. The fuzzy texture increases friction, helping the ball spin when it hits the court. The rubber is not airtight. After a few games, a tennis ball loses some air—and some of its bounce.

Table tennis

Lightest of all, this plastic shell filled with air travels fast—but not too fast. It's light enough so friction in air slows it to manageable speeds.

Bowling

A bowling ball, solid except for the finger holes, is heavy for its size. Usually made of hardened rubber, the ball has a smooth surface. The smoothness cuts down friction as the ball rolls down the alley. The heaviness gives the ball enormous inertia, which helps wallop the bowling pins and send them flying.

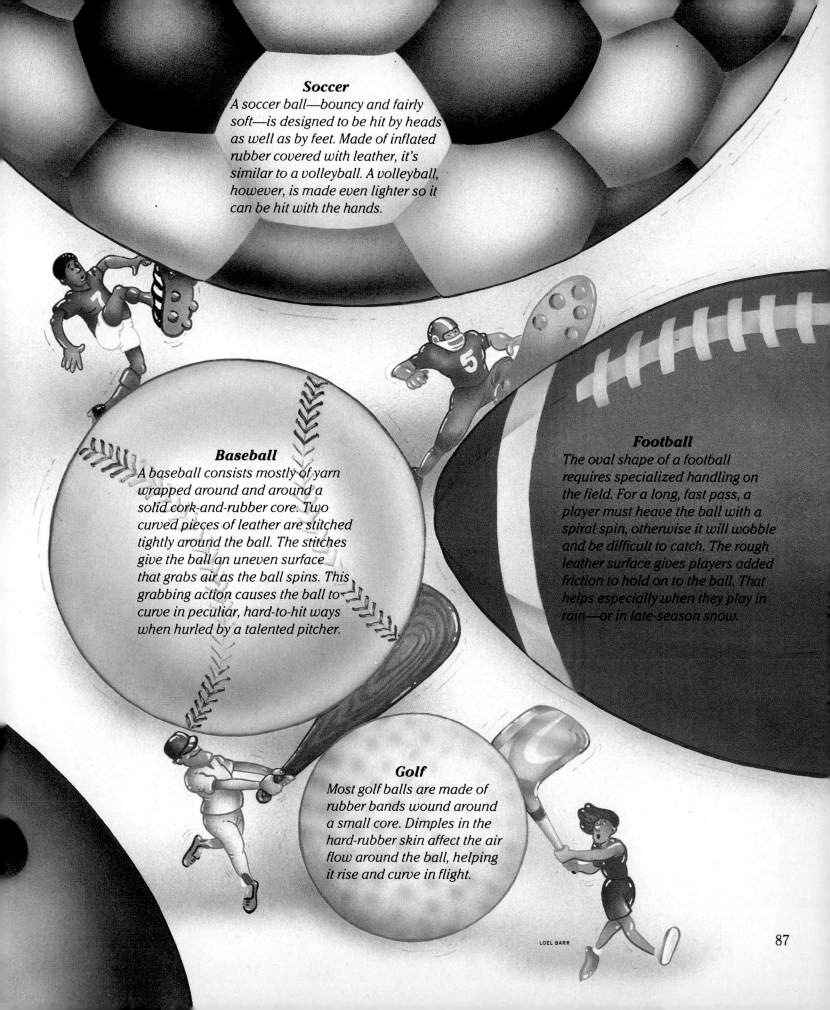

Soccer

A soccer ball—bouncy and fairly soft—is designed to be hit by heads as well as by feet. Made of inflated rubber covered with leather, it's similar to a volleyball. A volleyball, however, is made even lighter so it can be hit with the hands.

Baseball

A baseball consists mostly of yarn wrapped around and around a solid cork-and-rubber core. Two curved pieces of leather are stitched tightly around the ball. The stitches give the ball an uneven surface that grabs air as the ball spins. This grabbing action causes the ball to curve in peculiar, hard-to-hit ways when hurled by a talented pitcher.

Football

The oval shape of a football requires specialized handling on the field. For a long, fast pass, a player must heave the ball with a spiral spin, otherwise it will wobble and be difficult to catch. The rough leather surface gives players added friction to hold on to the ball. That helps especially when they play in rain—or in late-season snow.

Golf

Most golf balls are made of rubber bands wound around a small core. Dimples in the hard-rubber skin affect the air flow around the ball, helping it rise and curve in flight.

LOEL BARR

87

Bank on This

Have you ever noticed how some roads bank, or tilt inward, on tight turns? On such turns, steering and friction of the tires might not be enough to keep your car on the road. Inertia, the tendency to move in a straight line, could send you skidding off the curve. A banked turn helps push your car into the curve.

The force with which the banked curve of a road pushes you is called **centripetal** (sen-TRIP-uh-tul) **force**. You've seen that force in action in many other places. If you whirl a can on the end of a string, the string provides centripetal force that makes the can stay in a circle rather than fly off in a straight line.

Some people may speak of centrifugal (sen-TRIF-uh-gul) force, a force that causes things to fly to the outside of a circle. They say it presses you against the door of your car as you round a bend. But it only feels as if centrifugal force existed. What people call centrifugal force is actually inertia trying to make you go straight when *centripetal* force is pushing the car into the curve.

*As a skier leans into a tight turn, the edges of her skis cut into the snow. This creates tiny snowbanks under the skis that push her into the turn. The force that causes an object to turn in a circular path is called **centripetal force.** Here, the tiny snowbanks provide centripetal force for the skier. To keep from toppling over, the skier must lean in the direction of the centripetal force.*

RONALD C. MODRA/SPORTS ILLUSTRATED

Racing close to 90 miles an hour (145 km/h), a bobsled hurtles around an icy curve. Inertia tends to make the bobsled go straight. The sled needs a force to help turn it. Centripetal force provided by the steeply banked wall adds the necessary help.

If you ever visit the North Pole or South Pole, or any other very cold place, don't count on ice-skating. Your skates may not work.

Ice-skating normally works for one reason: When you put pressure on ice, it melts. As you step onto the ice with your skates, your weight presses down through the skate's thin blades. The ice directly under them melts just a bit. When skating, you slide on a thin film of melted ice.

Why couldn't you skate at the North Pole? In colder and colder weather, you need greater and greater weight to melt ice. Once the temperature goes below –8°F (–22°C), nobody is heavy enough to melt ice—and ice skates won't slide.

Snowball making, too, is possible because ice melts under pressure. When you compress snow, some of it melts. The moistened snowflakes stick together, and you have a snowball. When you take the pressure off, the melted snow turns back to ice. This refreezing process is called regelation (ree-juh-LAY-shun). Because you didn't heat the snowball, the water in it freezes again shortly after you take the pressure off. (You can't make snowballs in very cold weather. The snow will stay powdery.)

The Fine Line Between Ice and Water

Try it!

Watch a wire melt ice as a skate blade does. Take two spoons and a ruler-length thin wire. Wrap each end of the wire around a spoon, leaving 4 inches (10 cm) between the spoons. Now place an ice cube on top of an open bottle. Lay the wire across the ice and pull down slowly but steadily on the spoons. The pressure of the wire should make the wire melt a narrow channel all the way through the ice.

LOEL BARR

▲ *Tuesday Dawson, 13, glides in a San Francisco rink with all her weight concentrated on her skate blade. The great pressure of the thin blade melts the ice directly under it. The thin film of water under the blade lubricates the metal and the ice, allowing Tuesday to glide with reduced friction across the ice.*

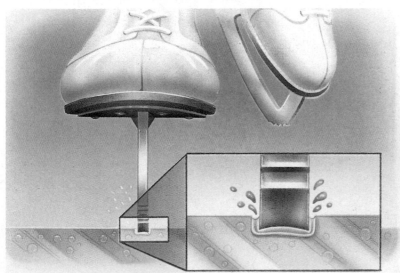

STEPHEN R. WAGNER

▲ *A closeup view of an ice skate shows why the narrow blade glides on ice. Because the blade supports the whole weight of the skater, it puts a lot of pressure on a small area. Ice melts under pressure. As the blade melts a slippery channel, the skater slides across the ice on a thin layer of water. Materials such as clay and steel do not melt under pressure, so you can't "ice-skate" on them.*

ROGER RESSMEYER (OPPOSITE)

91

Wired to Touch

The sport of fencing, shown here, may look unfamiliar. But the electrical system it uses for scoring should not be unfamiliar. It works exactly as home electrical systems work. In order for any electrical appliance to work, you must have an **electric circuit.**

An electric circuit is a complete loop or path that carries electric current. It goes from a power source to an appliance and back to the source. For an electrical appliance to run, the circuit must be complete. Break the circuit, and the appliance shuts off.

In your kitchen, the plug for a wall clock has two prongs. When you plug in the clock, you complete a circuit. Electrons race through one prong and one wire into the clock. In the clock, they power a small motor. The electrons continue through the clock and out another wire into the other prong. Pulling the plug out will break the circuit. The clock will stop running.

Chris Reuter, on the right, scores a point by touching Andrew Stifel with the tip of his épée (EH-pay). An épée is a sword used in the sport of fencing. As the ancient sport is practiced today, fencers do not inflict injury. The two Maryland 17-year-olds—Chris, from Bethesda, and Andrew, from Kensington—practice with a modern touch, an electrical scoring system. Wires under their jackets form part of an **electric circuit,** *or loop. The épées are part of the circuit. When a fencer touches an opponent with the épée, a switch on the tip completes the circuit, signaling a score.*

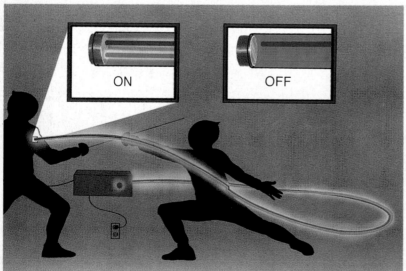

ON	OFF

BARBARA L. GIBSON

The tip of an épée holds a switch. Normally, the switch is open. Score a touch, and the tip is pressed in, closing the switch and completing the circuit. Current flows through the circuit, turning on a light and sounding a buzzer.

Action/Reaction

As you learn about physics, you may come across a principle that you just don't believe. To many people, Newton's third law of motion is one of those stumpers. The third law states that for every action, there is an equal and opposite reaction. According to Newton, if you push against a wall, at the same time that you move away from the wall, the wall moves away from you. Hard to believe? It's true, but the movement is too small to measure.

You've probably seen many films of a rocket taking off. As the fuel ignites, it starts to produce expanding gases that push out in all directions. The gases can escape only from the rear of the rocket. As the flaming gases are pushed out the rear of the rocket, the rocket is pushed skyward.

The next time you race a friend across a swimming pool, you're sure to observe Newton's third law. When you use your arms to push the water back, the water moves in that direction, and you move forward.

There are many things you couldn't do without Newton's third law of motion. Physics is like that. You can't get along without it.

TED SPIEGEL/BLACK STAR

When a crew team pulls on the oars attached to the boat, the large, flat blades of the oars push against the water. Isaac Newton pointed out that any force has two effects. In this case, when a force is exerted on the oar, it acts on the water. It also acts in an opposite direction on the boat. One force makes the water and the boat move in opposite directions. Physicists refer to this relationship of effects as **action and reaction.**

PETER READ MILLER

◀ *Charging into a race, sprinters push hard against their starting blocks. According to Newton's third law of motion, as each runner pushes off, the planet earth and the starting block attached are pushed back— but not enough to measure. At the same time, the runner is pushed forward. The runner and the earth are pushed in opposite directions. The earth is so large compared with a runner that it really barely moves when the runner pushes. Just about all of the motion is concentrated in the runner, sending her off down the track.*

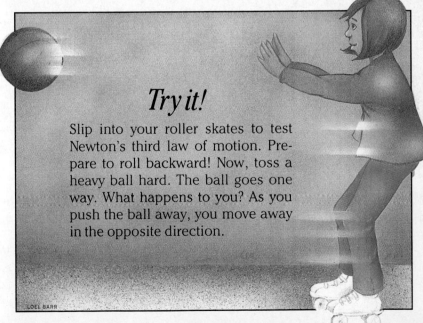

Try it!

Slip into your roller skates to test Newton's third law of motion. Prepare to roll backward! Now, toss a heavy ball hard. The ball goes one way. What happens to you? As you push the ball away, you move away in the opposite direction.

LOEL BARR

95

Physics Fun

Anti-gravity Ball

Things you will need:
Round, wide-mouthed jar   Table-tennis ball

What to do:
Place the jar upside down over the ball on a work table or kitchen table. Start to rotate the jar rapidly. The ball should move around the edge of the jar and start climbing inside as it swirls around. Keep swirling, and slowly lift the jar off the table.

Physics at work:
Why does the ball stay inside the lip of the jar instead of dropping out? Centripetal force is at work here. As you swirl the jar, inertia tries to make the ball go in a straight line. The jar applies the centripetal force, forcing the ball to travel in a circle. The ball's tendency to move outward keeps it above the lip of the jar.

Go, Balloons!

Things you will need:
Each of two or more persons will need:
Balloon	String
Plastic straw	Masking tape

What to do:
Choose two straight trees about 15 feet (5 m) apart. Tie one end of the string to one tree, and push the loose end through a straw. Now tie the other end to the other tree. Have your friends do the same with their strings, leaving about a foot (30 cm) between each string. Now blow up your balloon and ask a friend to tape it to the straw while you continue to pinch the end of the balloon shut. When your friends have all done the same, you're ready to race. The first balloon to the other tree wins. On your marks, get set, let go!

Physics at work:
When you let go of the balloon, Newton's third law of motion operates. ("Every action has an equal and opposite reaction.") The balloon squeezes the air and the air rushes out the balloon's opening. As the air rushes out the back, the balloon slides forward along the string.

LOEL BARR

Lemon 'Juice'

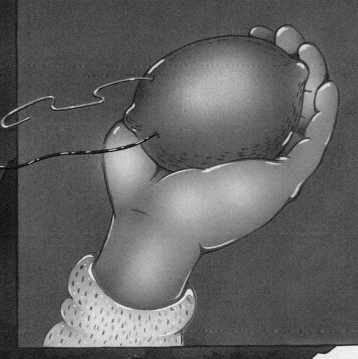

Things you will need:
Lemon
Short piece of copper wire
Steel paper clip

What to do:
Straighten the paper clip and poke one end through the rind into the lemon. Poke the copper wire into the lemon, too, near the paper clip but not touching it. Hold the ends of the wire and the clip close together and touch them both to your tongue. Do you feel a tingle?

Physics at work:
The lemon juice provides a path for the exchange of electrons between the two wires. Your wet tongue completes the circuit for the flow of electrons, and current flows across your tongue. You feel the current as a tiny tingle.

'Eggs-periment'

Things you will need:
Raw egg   Hard-boiled egg

What to do:
Spin the hard-boiled egg on a tabletop. Let it turn for a moment, then stop it and *immediately* release it. Do the same with the raw egg. One of the eggs should start turning—just a little—after you release it. Which one? Why?

Physics at work:
The raw egg will start to spin again because it has a liquid center. Even when you stop that egg from spinning, inertia keeps the liquid inside turning because it is not attached to the shell. When you release the shell, the spinning liquid starts the shell moving again.

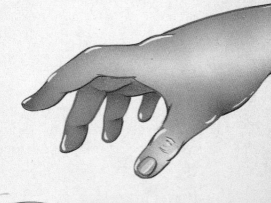

Standing Stopper

What to do:
Use a thimble or a pair of pliers to push the eye end of the needle into the end of the cork. Bend the wire into a semicircle. Push one end of the wire into the side of the cork and the other end into the apple. Rest the point of the needle near the edge of a work table or shelf. Bend the wire, if you need to, so that the cork stands up straight on the needle.

Physics at work:
What makes the cork and needle stand up? The device you built has a center of gravity in or near the heaviest part—the apple. The device balances, or stands up, when its center of gravity is directly under its point of support—the needle. Any hanging object is balanced when its center of gravity is directly below its point of support.

Balancing Match

What to do:
Carefully push the bowl of the spoon between the tines, or points, of the fork. The fork and spoon should form a wide *V* shape together. Insert the match into the fork, as shown, and hang the contraption on the edge of the glass. Do the fork and spoon appear to float in air? Adjust the match and the fork and spoon until they do balance as shown at right.

Physics at work:
There's no magic here. It's the center of gravity operating again. The center of gravity of the fork and spoon is somewhere between the handles of the two. It's not in the fork or in the spoon. The fork and spoon will balance on the match when their center of gravity lies directly below their point of support—the spot where the match rests on the glass.

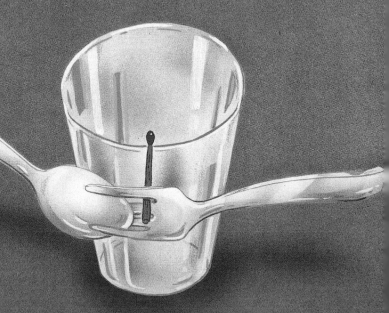

LOEL BARR

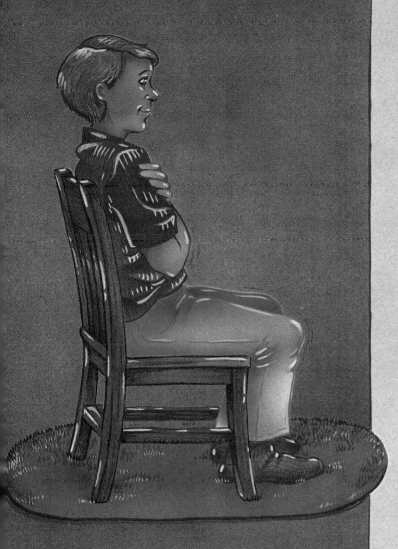

Bound to Balance

What you will need:
    Set of encyclopedias, or other volumes of the same size

What to do:
On the edge of a desk, stack the books, one overhanging the next. Each book should extend beyond the previous one. With seven or eight volumes, can you get the top book in the stack completely over the edge of the table? (Helpful hint: Don't slide the lower books as far over each other as the upper books.)

Physics at work:
Once again, the center of gravity is the key. The books will not fall if the center of gravity of any group of the books lies over the book supporting them. For example, if you have eight books in the stack, look at the top three—books eight, seven, and six. If the center of gravity of those three together lies above book five, book five will support them. If not, the top books will fall.

Glued to Your Seat

What you will need:
    Straight-backed chair

What to do:
Sit with your back flat against the chair back. Fold your arms in front of you. Can you stand up without leaning forward?

Physics at work:
Chances are, you stayed seated. In that position, your center of gravity is over the seat. To stand up, you have to lean forward, shifting your center of gravity over your feet.

GLOSSARY

On this page and the next, you will find definitions of words or terms that appear in the book in **bold type.**

Adhesion—(add-HEE-zhun) the force of attraction between the molecules of two different kinds of substances.

Alternating current (ac)—a flow of electrons that changes direction 60 times a second. Electricity provided to households is alternating current.

Angle of incidence—on a reflecting surface, the angle between the incoming light and an imaginary line straight out from the surface.

Angle of reflection—on a reflecting surface, the angle between the reflecting light and an imaginary line straight out from the surface.

Atmospheric pressure—pressure caused by the weight of the air that blankets the earth. Atmospheric pressure becomes less as you move higher above sea level.

Atom—the smallest whole part of an element. Atoms make up molecules. An atom has a nucleus, or center, circled by one or more electrons.

Aurora australis—a glowing, flickering curtain of light sometimes visible in the sky normally near the antarctic region. It is caused by electrically charged particles from the sun within the magnetic field of the earth.

Aurora borealis—a glowing, flickering curtain of light sometimes visible in the sky normally near the arctic region. It is caused by electrically charged particles from the sun within the magnetic field of the earth.

Bernoulli's principle—a law of physics: The pressure exerted by a fluid decreases as the fluid speeds up.

Buoyancy—(BOY-un-see) the ability of an object to float. A floating object weighs the same as the water it displaces.

Center of gravity—the place where the entire weight of an object appears to be concentrated.

Coherent (CO-HEAR-unt) **light**—light waves of one wavelength in perfect coordination. They shine brightly and for a long distance. Laser light is coherent light.

Cohesion—the force of attraction between molecules within a single kind of substance.

Compression—the part of a wavelength of sound where the molecules are pressed close together.

Compressional waves—waves, such as sound waves, that travel through a substance by moving molecules closer together and farther apart.

Condensation—the process by which a substance changes from a gas into a liquid.

Conductor—a material that transfers electric current or heat. Copper and aluminum are good conductors of both electricity and heat.

Crystal—a rigid structure of molecules making up a solid. Ice is an example of water crystals lumped together.

Deposition—the process by which a gas changes directly to a solid without first becoming a liquid.

Direct current (dc)—a steady flow of electrons, such as that which you get from a battery.

Echolocation—(ek-oh-low-KAY-shun) a system bats and certain other animals use for finding their way—and their food. A bat makes sounds, then uses the echoes to locate obstacles or prey.

Elastic energy—a kind of potential energy found in a substance that has been bent under force. Elastic energy will help return the substance to its original form when the force is removed.

Electric circuit—a complete loop of electrical conductors that includes an electrical source and often an electrical appliance.

Electromagnetic spectrum—the complete range of electromagnetic waves, including X rays, visible light, and radio and TV waves.

Electron—a negatively charged part of the atom that moves around the nucleus, or center, of the atom. A stream of electrons is an electric current.

Evaporation—the process by which a liquid changes state and turns into a gas.

Force—a push or pull on an object.

Frequency—one measurement of waves. It tells how many waves pass a given spot in one second.

Friction—the force that acts when two surfaces rub against each other. Friction tends to slow down objects or keep them from moving.

Fulcrum—the point on a lever where the lever pivots, or turns. The fulcrum can be at either end of a lever or somewhere between, depending on the kind of lever.

Gamma rays—the kind of electromagnetic waves that carry the most energy. Released by nuclear reactions, they can travel through most substances, including concrete.

Gravity—the force of attraction between any two objects in the universe that have mass, or substance. The strongest gravitational pull on you is from the earth.

Incoherent (in-co-HEAR-unt) **light**—unorganized light waves of different wavelengths. Incoherent light, such as that from a flashlight, spreads out and fades faster than coherent light, such as laser light.

Inertia—(in-ER-shuh) a property, or quality, that tends to keep a moving object in motion in a straight line, or to keep a motionless object at rest, unless either one is acted upon by an outside force.

Infrared (in-fruh-RED) **waves**—invisible electromagnetic waves that you can feel as heat.

Insulator—a material that absorbs energy and does not transfer it.

Iridescence—(ir-uh-DES-ents) bright, shiny color caused by the reflection, bending, and combining of light waves when they strike certain birds, butterflies, and minerals.

Kinetic (kuh-NET-ik) **energy**—energy of motion. Whenever you are moving, you automatically have kinetic energy from that motion.

Law of reflection—On a reflecting surface, the angle of the incoming light equals the angle of the reflected light.

Lever—a simple machine consisting of a bar that moves around a fixed point. You apply a force to one part of a lever, and another part of the lever moves something.

Lift—an upward force that results when the air pressure below a wing is greater than the air pressure above it. Lift makes it possible for birds and airplanes to fly.

Magnetic field—an area in which a magnetic force is in effect. A magnetic field curves from one pole of a magnet to the other, and is most concentrated near the poles.

Magnetic poles—on the earth, two spots, one near the North Pole and one near the South Pole, where the earth's magnetic field is most concentrated.

Microwaves—short-wavelength radio waves useful in satellite communications and in cooking food.

Molecule—the smallest pure particle of a substance, much smaller than the eye can see. Molecules are made up of atoms.

Non-Newtonian fluid—a fluid that behaves in some ways like a liquid and in some ways like a solid. Quicksand is a non-Newtonian fluid.

Normal—a line straight out from a reflecting surface. Angles of reflected light are measured from the normal.

Parabolic (par-uh-BAHL-ik) **arc**—a curve that describes the path of a hurled object when the object is affected by the force of gravity.

Photon—a tiny packet of electromagnetic radiation, or energy. In large numbers, they make up light.

Photovoltaic (fo-to-vahl-TAY-ik) **cell**—see *Solar cell.*

Pigments—chemicals that absorb some wavelengths of light and reflect others, which you see as colors.

Potential (puh-TEN-shul) **energy**—stored energy.

Prism—a piece of cut glass or other transparent material with at least three sides. A prism separates white light into the different colors that make up the white light.

Projectile—an object that travels through air or space not under its own power. A hurled object is a projectile.

Radio waves—electromagnetic waves useful in communication over distance.

Rarefaction—(rare-uh-FAK-shun) the part of a wavelength of sound in which the molecules are far apart from each other.

Resistance—the action by which a substance resists movement.

Scattering—the process by which the sun's rays hit tiny particles in the atmosphere and bounce off in all directions, causing the sky to appear blue or reddish, depending upon the time of day.

Simple harmonic motion—any repeating motion with a regular repetition time. The pendulum in a grandfather clock moves with simple harmonic motion.

Solar cell—a manufactured device of wires and layers of silicon in which sunlight stimulates the movement of electrons to produce electricity. Also known as a photovoltaic cell.

Spectrum—in physics, the range of wavelengths of electromagnetic radiation. A rainbow shows a small part of the spectrum—the colors that make up visible light.

Static electricity—a collection of unbalanced (positive or negative) electrical charges that build up in one place, such as in a cloud.

Surface tension—the tendency of a liquid to hold together at its surface as if it had a skin.

Transformer—a device used to decrease or increase electrical voltage.

Viscosity— (viss-KAHS-uht-ee) internal friction in a liquid caused by the molecules of the liquid rubbing together. A liquid with high viscosity, such as honey, flows slowly.

Water vapor—water in the form of a gas. Steam is water vapor.

Wavelength—the distance between one wave crest, or peak, and the next. The wavelength of a light wave determines its color. The wavelength of a sound wave determines the tone you hear.

Ultraviolet rays—light waves invisible to humans, but visible to most insects. Ultraviolet rays cause sunburn.

Visible light—a small part of the electromagnetic spectrum, consisting of wavelengths of light that you can see, including all the colors of the rainbow.

X rays—invisible electromagnetic rays useful in making photographs of teeth and bones.

INDEX

ALAN BECKER

Physicist Ilan Chabay and students at the Aspen Community School, in Colorado, marvel at the brilliant colors of soap bubbles. There's a lot to question about soap bubbles. What holds them together? Why do their colors shimmer? Why do they reflect the photographer's lights? Why, it's physics, naturally!

SCIENCE MUSEUMS

For more fun with physics, visit one of these science museums near your home, or plan to see some on your next trip.

1. Alberta Natural Resources Science Centre, Strathcona Science Park, P.O. Box 3182, **Sherwood Park, Alberta, Canada** T8A 2A6. **2.** Center of Science and Industry, 280 East Broad Street, **Columbus, Ohio** 43215–3773. **3.** The Children's Discovery Museum, 177 Main Street, **Acton, Massachusetts** 01720. **4.** The Children's Museum, 30th and Meridian Streets, **Indianapolis, Indiana** 46205. **5.** Cleveland Children's Museum, 10730 Euclid Avenue, **Cleveland, Ohio** 44106. **6.** Detroit Science Center, 5020 John R Street, **Detroit, Michigan** 48202. **7.** The Exploratorium, 3601 Lyon Street, **San Francisco, California** 94123. **8.** The Exploreum, 1906 Springhill Avenue, **Mobile, Alabama** 36607. **9.** The Franklin Institute Science Museum, 20th and The Parkway, **Philadelphia, Pennsylvania** 19103. **10.** Jacksonville Museum of Arts and Sciences, 1025 Gulf Life Drive, **Jacksonville, Florida** 32207. **11.** Louisiana Nature and Science Center, Inc., 11000 Lake Forest Blvd., **New Orleans, Louisiana** 70127–2816. **12.** The Magic House, 516 S. Kirkwood Road, **Kirkwood, Missouri** 63122. **13.** Impression 5, Michigan's Science Museum, 200 Museum Drive, **Lansing, Michigan** 48933. **14.** Museum of Science and Industry, 57th Street and Lake Shore Drive, **Chicago, Illinois** 60637. **15.** Museum of Science, Economics and Technology, Inc./Discovery World, 818 West Wisconsin Avenue, **Milwaukee, Wisconsin** 53233. **16.** The Omaha Children's Museum, 551 South 18th Street, **Omaha, Nebraska** 68102. **17.** Omniplex Science and Arts Museum, 2100 N.E. 52nd Street, in Kirkpatrick Center, **Oklahoma City, Oklahoma** 73111. **18.** Ontario Science Centre, 770 Don Mills Road, **Don Mills, Ontario, Canada** M3C IT3. **19.** Oregon Museum of Science and Industry, 4015 S. W. Canyon Road, **Portland, Oregon** 97221. **20.** The Science Museum of Minnesota, 30 East 10th Street, **St. Paul, Minnesota** 55101. **21.** St. Louis Science Center, 5050 Oakland Avenue, **St. Louis, Missouri** 63110.

DENNIS HAMILTON, JR.

COVER: *Mike Britt, 14, of Green Cove Springs, Florida, lays his hands on a Van de Graaff generator. The generator produces strong, negative electrical charges in the silver sphere. When Mike touches it, the negative charges race through his body. Negative charges push away one another, and so Mike's hair stands on end— each hair as far away from the others as it can get. The charge tingles, but it doesn't hurt.*

ADDITIONAL READING

General Reading: Kent, Amanda, and Alan Ward, *Introduction To Physics—A Simple Introduction for Beginners,* Usborne Publishing, Ltd., London, 1983 • National Geographic Society, *How Things Work,* Washington, D. C. 1983. **Books on Specific Subjects:** Cole, K. C., *Facets of Light: Colors, Images, and Things that Glow in the Dark,* The Exploratorium, San Francisco, 1980 • Simon, Seymour, *The Paper Airplane Book,* Penguin Books, New York, 1985 • Walther, Tom, *Make Mine Music!,* Little, Brown and Company, Boston, 1981. **Physics Crafts:** Cobb, Vicki, and Kathy Darling, *Bet You Can! Science Possibilities to Fool You,* Avon Books, New York, 1983 • Herbert, Don, and Hy Ruchlis, *Mr. Wizard's 400 Experiments in Science,* Book-Lab, New Jersey, 1983 • Science Club series: *Amazing Air; Light Fantastic; Liquid Magic; Super Motion;* Lothrop, Lee & Shepard Books, New York, 1982.

EDUCATIONAL CONSULTANTS

Andrew J. Pogan, Science Department Chairman, Gaithersburg High School, Maryland; Richard E. Berg, Ph.D., Department of Physics, University of Maryland, *Chief Consultants*
Glenn O. Blough, LL.D., Emeritus Professor of Education, University of Maryland, *Educational Consultant*
Julia W. Tossell, M.D., *Consulting Psychiatrist*
Linda Bush, Montgomery County (Maryland) Public Schools, *Reading Consultant*

The Special Publications and School Services Division is also grateful to the individuals and institutions named or quoted in the text and to those cited here for their generous assistance:

Lila Adair, Central Gwinnett High School, Lawrenceville, Ga.; Don Berkowitz, Georgia Institute of Technology; Peter Brancazio, Brooklyn College; Scott Britt and Clay Frazier, Georgia Stone Mountain State Park; Jim Brownell, Falls Church, Va.; Tim Casey, Rutgers University; Raymon Davie, Ardsley Middle School, Ardsley, N.Y.; Edgar A. DeMeo, Electric Power Research Institute, Palo Alto, Ca.; John Dreyer, Walt Disney World Epcot Center, Florida; Alistair B. Fraser, Pennsylvania State University; Howard C. Gerhardt, University of Missouri; Robert L. Gluck, Washington, D. C.; Robert Greenler, University of Wisconsin; Lynn W. Kinnie, Fun City, Estes Park, Colo.

Robert N. Little, University of Texas. Paul Maycock, PV Energy Systems, Inc., Casanova, Va.; Larry Nyce, American University, Washington, D. C.; Joe O'Donnell, San Francisco; Clifford E. Swartz, State University of New York at Stonybrook; Merlin D. Tuttle, Bat Conservation International, Inc.; Jearl Walker, Cleveland State University; David A. West, Virginia Polytechnic Institute; Jack M. Wilson, American Association of Physics Teachers.

Gratitude for assistance in testing the activities goes to Betty, Christopher, and Matthew Behnke; Jim and Jeff Bullard; Mark Carlson; Sandy Crow; Caroline, Ken, and Melanie Danforth; Pat and Shannon Foor; Joe and Seth Fowler; Alexandra, Christopher, and Martha George; Derek, Mary, and Stephen Lamberton; Laura Liddell and her students, Camelot School, Annandale, Va.; Joe Mettenburg; Andrea, Keith, and Melissa Moorehead; Jonathan and Suzanne Patrick; Sean Peters; Katie Robeson; Cynthia, Katie, and Nelse Winder; Karen Yee; Matthew Zopf.

Composition for FUN WITH PHYSICS! by National Geographic's Photographic Services, Carl M. Shrader, Director; Lawrence F. Ludwig, Assistant Director. Printed and bound by Holladay-Tyler Printing Corp., Rockville, Md. Film preparation by Catharine Cooke Studio, Inc., New York, N.Y. Color separations by Lincoln Graphics, Inc., Cherry Hill, N.J.; and NEC, Inc., Nashville, Tenn. Teacher's Guide printed by McCollum Press, Inc., Rockville, Md.

Library of Congress CIP Data

McGrath, Susan, 1955–
    Fun with physics.
    (Books for world explorers)
    Bibliography: p.
    Includes index.
    Summary: Explains how physics is involved in all aspects of our lives—through chapters on physics in fun, nature, home, and sports—and presents activities to demonstrate physical principles.
    1. Physics—Juvenile literature. [1. Physics]
I. Title. II. Series.
QC25.M24   1986   530   86-8501
ISBN 0-87044-576-6 (regular edition)
ISBN 0-87044-581-2 (library edition)

FUN WITH PHYSICS
by Susan McGrath

PUBLISHED BY
THE NATIONAL GEOGRAPHIC SOCIETY
WASHINGTON, D. C.

Gilbert M. Grosvenor, *President*
Melvin M. Payne, *Chairman of the Board*
Owen R. Anderson, *Executive Vice President*
Robert L. Breeden, *Senior Vice President, Publications and Educational Media*

PREPARED BY THE SPECIAL PUBLICATIONS
AND SCHOOL SERVICES DIVISION

Donald J. Crump, *Director*
Philip B. Silcott, *Associate Director*
Bonnie S. Lawrence, *Assistant Director*

BOOKS FOR WORLD EXPLORERS
Pat Robbins, *Editor*
Ralph Gray, *Editor Emeritus*
Ursula Perrin Vosseler, *Art Director*
David P. Johnson, *Illustrations Editor*
Margaret McKelway, *Associate Editor*

STAFF FOR *FUN WITH PHYSICS*
Roger B. Hirschland, *Managing Editor*
Charles M. Kogod, *Picture Editor*
Louise Ponsford, *Art Director*
M. Barbara Brownell, *Researcher*
Loel Barr, Sharon A. Davis, Barbara L. Gibson,
Stephen R. Wagner, *Artists*
Patricia N. Holland, *Special Projects Editor*
Carol R. Curtis, Lori Elizabeth Davie,
Editorial Assistants
Artemis S. Lampathakis, *Senior Illustrations Assistant*
Bernadette L. Grigonis, *Illustrations Assistant*

ENGRAVING, PRINTING, AND PRODUCT MANUFACTURE: Robert W. Messer, *Manager;* David V. Showers, *Production Manager;* Gregory Storer, *Production Project Manager;* George J. Zeller, Jr., *Senior Assistant Production Manager;* Mark R. Dunlevy, *Assistant Production Manager;* Timothy H. Ewing, *Production Assistant.*

STAFF ASSISTANTS: Mary F. Brennan, Vicki L. Broom, Katherine R. Davenport, Mary Elizabeth Davis, Ann Di Fiore, Rosamund Garner, Virginia W. Hannasch, Nancy J. Harvey, Joan Hurst, Ann E. Newman, Cleo Petroff, Stuart E. Pfitzinger, Virginia A. Williams.

MARKET RESEARCH: Mark W. Brown, Joseph S. Fowler, Carrla L. Holmes, Marla Lewis, Barbara Steinwurtzel, Marsha Sussman, Judy Turnbull.

INDEX: James B. Enzinna